JUPITER'S RINGS

JUPITER'S RINGS

Balance from the Inside Out

Howard Schechter

WHITE CLOUD PRESS

ASHLAND, OREGON

Printed in Indonesia

First edition: 2002

Cover design: David Rupee, Impact Publications

ISBN: 1-883991-40-4

TABLE OF CONTENTS

Thank you Barbara Lee
for your kind and loving support.

CHAPTER ONE

Harmony Within,
Balance Without

MYTHOLOGICALLY, JUPITER symbolizes expansion—under
standing through the development of consciousness. Jupiter
has been known to us since the ancients first stared into the sky and
felt the awe of the night heavens. In the history of science, Jupiter
was the first planet Galileo studied when he turned his telescope to
the sky to chart the spheres.

The rings of Jupiter, however, have been unknown to us until
recently. They were discovered in 1979 during a flyby of the planet
by the spacecraft Voyager. Photographs taken ten years later, in 1989,
by the spacecraft Galileo, show Jupiter's rings to be even more glo-
riously beautiful than originally thought. These outer manifestations
of the planet are composed of dust generated from the inner moons.

The metaphor of Jupiter and its rings for our lives is powerful.
It is through the growth of consciousness, the constant refining of
our inner process, that our external lives unfold in beauty and balance, exemplified by Jupiter's rings. Though the planet and it's symbolism of expanded consciousness has been known and honored

throughout the ages by the few, it is only recently, in the discovery of Jupiter's rings, that a powerful and moving emblem has been created for the many to recognize that it is time to understand the fundamental principle: a life in balance is an inside job.

Saturn is the planet we commonly associate with rings. Interestingly, Saturn is the planet which symbolizes external ordering, organization, restriction, discipline, and rigidity. These are the strategies we habitually and without examination turn to when the discomfort of imbalance in our lives drives us into seeking change. Unfortunately, Saturnine strategies seldom work. They do not endure long enough to create real change nor balance. And, unfortunately, when the attempt to reorder the external components of our lives fails we are left not only in a continuing state of disequilibrium but with a sense of hopelessness that achieving balance is impossible.

This book presents an alternative—a methodology which focuses on the growth of consciousness. Inner work, both spiritual and psychological, will result in the flowering, beauty, and balance of our external lives. The metaphor of Jupiter and it's rings becomes even more powerful when we add the very recent scientific evidence that Jupiter has served as protection for Earth since the beginning of time. Jupiter's massive gravity acts as a shield protecting our home planet from collisions with asteroids and comets capable of ending life as we know it. Further, massive Jupiter, the friendly giant into which all the other planets in our solar system can fit, has a powerfully stable orbit which keeps our planet's orbit in balance, a safe distance from the sun. The inner work we do for ourselves—described, discussed and demonstrated below will keep our personal orbit stable and in balance as well.

In her biography, *Jung: His Life and Work*, Barbara Hannah relates a story told by the great psychiatrist Carl Jung about Richard Wilhelm. Wilhelm was in a remote Chinese village that was experiencing a terrible drought. The villagers had tried numerous methods to induce rain with no success. And so they sent for a wise old Rainmaker from a faraway village in hope that he could end the drought. Upon his arrival, the old man "sniffed the air in distaste" and immediately secluded himself in a cottage on the outskirts of town. After three days it began to rain and the crops were saved.

Wilhelm was greatly impressed and sought out the Rainmaker who had now come out of his seclusion. Wilhelm asked him in wonder: "So you can make rain?" The old man scoffed at the very idea and said of course he could not. "But, there was a most persistent drought until you came," Wilhelm retorted, "and then—within three days—it rains?" "Oh," replied the old man, "that was something quite different. You see, I come from a region where everything is in order, it rains when it should and is fine when that is needed, and the people are also in order and in themselves. But that was not the case with the people here, they were all out of Tao (Balance) and out of themselves. I was at once infected when I arrived, so I had to be quite alone until I was once more in Tao and then naturally it rained." [1]

Like the Chinese villagers, we too are in need of restoring equilibrium to our lives. There is a great yearning for balance in our present age of anxiety and acceleration. With the pace of life quickened by technology, stressed by the workplace, and pressurized by relationship, a widespread longing for a better way is observable Many of us are looking for an approach to living that will bring more joy and satisfaction in the midst of what feels like the jumble of modern life.

Modern western culture values the material as more important than the spiritual; the intellectual over the emotional. As a result, we are out of balance; science and technology have almost won the "war against nature." In the process we are losing our selves; and the victory is hollow and many are exhausted.

There is a better way, and it does not involve the loss of what we have already gained in material abundance. It is a way that adds, not subtracts, and involves the awakening of Spirit and the honoring of emotion. Integrated into our already well-developed mental and material capacities, the renewal of Spirit and unfreezing of our emotional intelligence can create an internal harmony that will lead to the external balance we are seeking.

The underlying assumptions of this book flow out of a spiritually-oriented psychology. Fundamentally, if we wish to achieve balance, we must nurture both our spiritual identity and our emotional

---

1. Cited in Barbara Hannah, *Jung: His Life and Work* (Wilmette, Ill.: Chiron Publications, 1997).

life. As the Taoists sages teach, each of us is already perfect. Beneath our socially-constructed personality, at the level of the "uncarved block," we are flawless. It is only our social and personal histories that interfere with remembering who we truly are.

From different yet complimentary spiritual perspectives, Hindu and Christian sages teach that even within this human realm of apparent imperfection we are all on a constantly evolving journey toward redemption. Our problems, our mistakes, our side journeys are not errors at all, but a pilgrimage towards wholeness.

Balance implies equalizing opposites, correct proportion, proper function, stability, and order. If we focus more fully and skillfully on developing our interior Self and inner harmony, then the outcome would naturally be a reflection of this: beauty; proportion, and order in the various aspects of our external lives.

Balance is central to the achievement of happiness. It is a critical aspect of the proper functioning of many human endeavors including the most hallowed of our time, science. As the principle upon which equations are based, balance is the foundation for much of mathematics, chemistry, physics and all the other physical sciences. Harmony and balance are generally considered defining aspects of beauty in the arts, the measure of grace in painting, music, literature and dance. Balance is crucial to the successful execution of sport and other physical activities. Harmony and balance are major themes in the macroeconomics of nations and the microeconomics of homes. They are primary principles for good health. It is no wonder that the great spiritual traditions world over extol what Buddhists call the "middle way."

External balance, however, is not simply moderation. It is the equalization of opposing forces. The weight on both ends of a scale may be extreme, but if they are equal, there is balance. Balance is not the absence of excess, just as peace is not the absence of war. It is far more, and balance has a positive additive quality that integrates contrasting forces into a stabilized unity.

Leading a life of balance is not about getting rid of anything. The "getting rid of" strategy seldom works. It is an external solution to an internal problem. Though the injunction "just let go" appears to be easy—even hip—in practice it is almost impossible. It fosters a sense of failure and harmful self-judgment. A more effective strategy is to cultivate inner harmony. Undesirable behaviors often drop away of their own accord as a result of the quality of serenity that develops.

For example, if we find ourselves worrying to the point of distraction, the command "stop worrying" is at best useless. It sounds good, in the same way that New Year's Eve resolutions are appealing but generally ineffectual. They are easy to make, satisfying for a short time, but overall create more conflict in the long run.

But if we slow down, become quiet, perhaps take a walk, we will be much better off. These activities dissipate the stored up energy that drives worry and, at the same time, cultivates inner harmony. Through this process, we notice an immediate diminishment in anxiety, a sense of freshness; often resulting in new insights and the power for making necessary and proper changes.

Balance is not a static quality or an end state that we finally achieve in order to rest peacefully within its embrace. Balance is a continuously unfolding process, wonderfully dynamic. In an integrated life we constantly move through balance; into it, out of it, and back into it again, endlessly. This motion is like a teeter-totter, each end an opposing quality, and we, the inner Self, are the fulcrum upon which it is balanced. The emphasis is on this fulcrum (inner har-

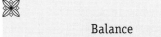

Balance
is more than Temperance

We have learned Temperance
Moderation
"don't go too far"

Neither exhilarates
neither uplifts

Balance exhilarates
Balance uplifts

Temperance
Moderation,
Negativity

Temperance calls
"give up"
"quit"
"fear the pleasure"

Balance calls,
"do it, be free"

It's hard to practice Balance
when we have learned Moderation

It gets in the way

mony) and the action (outer dynamic balance) flows from it but is not a static state.

It is really about the movement of *balancing* more than the state of *balance*. Like the moon, it is always changing, moving through phases, returning to fullness.

I recently led a series of workshops for executives and top sales producers with a large Philadelphia-based financial institution. The workshop was called "Balancing Act: Integrating Work and Family Life." What impressed me in these encounters was the severe pain people were feeling. The irony was the presence of so much guilt, dissatisfaction, futility and powerlessness in a group of apparently self-confident high achievers.

Initially, participants complained about the lack of balance between their work and family life. As we explored the issue further, it became clear to everyone that this imbalance in their outer lives was a reflection of internal disharmony. The discomfort they were experiencing in various external dimensions of their lives was deeply rooted in an inner discord they had not previously been fully aware of.

These people made a startling discovery that is becoming increasingly apparent to many: we are nurturing our selves even less than we are nurturing our families. No matter how much we wish to improve our lives, they will not really shift until we address the origin of the imbalance.

Despite outward success, these prosperous people never felt it was enough. No matter how many well intentioned resolutions these self-starters made, it did not result in a balanced life. A deep seated and pervasive sense of loss and sadness marked their lives. Life seemed to be slipping by, and the material trappings simply did not fill the emptiness.

It is hopeful that a significant proportion of the population is developing the consciousness necessary to adapt to our fast paced times. Bill Moyers, the popular television personality, has said that in his travels around the country the subject he finds people most interested in and enthusiastic about is spirituality. Similarly, a large scale survey by sociologist Paul H. Ray, commissioned by the Institute for Noetic Sciences, shows that 24% of all American adults, or 44 million people, are what Ray calls "transmodern" or "culturally creative": they are people who hold the values of spirituality, ecology, social consciousness, self development, authenticity and relationship most highly (*Noetic Sciences Review*, Spring 1996).

If the survey data is correct, one quarter of the population is already making progress in the effort to harmonize themselves, which would bring a more balanced nation into the 21st century.

From a systems perspective, this cultural movement toward balance is to be expected. In general, large systems tend to approach equilibrium in a dynamic way, moving in and out of balance. When off center, forces are generated within systems that draw them back toward equilibrium. The perfection lies in the fact that macroscopic forces at the system level support microscopic forces at the personal level which help us return to inner harmony and outer balance.

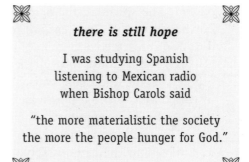

there is still hope

I was studying Spanish
listening to Mexican radio
when Bishop Carols said

"the more materialistic the society
the more the people hunger for God."

Harmony and balance are inner and outer aspects of the same phenomenon, the components of our lives The inner aspect, harmony, is the fulcrum upon which the balance bar rests. The outer aspect, balance itself, is the resultant quality. Harmony refers to our emotional and spiritual condition. Balance is the way in which we integrate the external aspects of our lives; work and play, family and friends, activity and relaxation, church and community, into a well proportioned, satisfying whole.

Though the internal and external elements interact to support or inhibit each other, internal harmony has primacy. It is the foundation upon which the external components rest. It is the source from which the flower of balance grows.

Harmony functions at the level of cause. Balance is an external mirror of the inner state. Harmony is like the sun, it has originating energy. Balance is like the moon, it is reflective.

Though outer balance supports the growth of inner harmony, as the atmosphere creates conditions for healthy plant growth, it is difficult to affect change by shifting external behavior alone. Effective solutions and changes must address problems at their roots. For a successful cure, the source must be treated. Our primary energy must flow toward developing internal harmony so that our outer life reflects this beauty.

What does it take to develop this internal harmony? According to the psychology of Carl Jung, four core elements define the whole person. The spiritual, the emotional, the mental and the physical. For harmony to be present, all four elements must be healthy, active, and integrated.

As I see it, these four elements, are not equal. Spirit is at the center. It is the dominant, causal, and controlling factor. The extent to which our spiritual house is in order largely determines the extent to which our emotional, mental and physical houses will be in order. Tragically, in western industrialized societies, this is often the least developed part of our selves.

a socio-spiritual commentary

why so much violence in the movies?
because as a culture
we are Soul Dead
ignorant of, resistant to
the sacred

we have forgotten the obvious truth
that indigenous peoples have known everywhere
since the beginning

there is a Mystery
and it is Sacred beyond our understanding

call it God or Chopped Liver
we need the fullness of Spirit

Spirit unites the Cosmos

most of us Know
though it's often hidden
under layers of cynicism
that there is a Force
greater than we
that science will never name

to attempt a society
based on materialism alone
is foolish

like trying to breath air in a vacuum.
denying the obvious truth

we gorge on over-stimulation
the Red-eyed Monster
hoping to fill the hole

constantly seeking satisfaction
never satisfied

violence is the symptom
Emptiness is the cause

CHAPTER TWO

An Unfettered Spirituality

Know ye not that
ye are the temple of
God, and that the Spirit of God
dwelleth in you.
I. Corinthians, 3:16

THERE IS A HALF CIRCLE embedded in the symbol of the planet Jupiter. This image represents the aspiration toward higher consciousness. A fundamental cause of human discord is the lack of spiritual focus in our lives. For most people, spirituality is directly connected to and identified with organized religion. However, social and economic abuses committed by institutionalized religion along with the disinformation historically perpetuated by clergy the world over, has turned many people against religion. The lack of depth and absence of true spirituality within traditional religious services has alienated even more. In the process of distancing ourselves from both the institutionalized abuses of religion and the lack of Spirit in the church, we have lost the benefit of religion's core purpose; providing a structure and process to help us access the Divine. It is the classic case of "throwing out the baby with the bath water." As noted in chapter one, this religious state of affairs has led to an radical shift in our culture with growing numbers of individuals seeking spiritual sustenance outside of traditional religious organizations, drawing selectively on various sources of wisdom to create a personal spiritual path.

Another reason for this pervasive alienation from our spiritual center is the dominant conception in Western culture concerning the nature of God. The traditional image of God is simplistic and anthropomorphic. God is defined as a person-like Being, residing in the heavens, responsible for and directing the events on earth. Prayer is the act of petitioning of this super Being to move events in the direction we desire.

This deeply rooted and unexamined assumption about the nature of God is typified by a U.S. congressman I heard on the radio, speaking about a flood disaster in his home state: "I don't know what we will do. But I know one thing, *God will figure it out. He always does.*" The background assumption is that there is a "he" in "heaven," "figuring things out" and then "doing something to fix it." Because this concept of a super Being moving people and events around like chess pieces on a board is so inconsistent with how we actually experience reality, it borders on the absurd.

Based upon these inadequacies and absurdities, most sensitive and thinking people end up rejecting religion and as a result rejecting spirituality.

Our actual experience, however, tells us that there is something greater than us, more grand and beyond our understanding. A creative principle, an infinite force, a divine mystery. We experience the mystery all the time. It comes particularly clear in the wonder of nature. Walking in the woods, listening to the flow of a river, shouting from a mountain top and hearing the echo reverberate and return. As children, before the element of mind becomes so dominant, we feel and dwell in the mystery. We still feel and know it in the presence of the awesome.

The poet John Keats has written, "Nothing becomes real until it is experienced. Even a proverb is no proverb until your life has illustrated it." We have experienced the great mystery and our lives have illustrated it, yet having rejected the traditional notion of God as super Being, we are left confused. Though we do experience a phenomenon that might better be called God-force or God-principle, it is not "provable" to the intellect. Given the cultural dominance of the scientific paradigm, which accepts as truth only that which is measurable by the senses, we continue to reject Spirit. Because it is not observable through the physical senses, not quantifiable nor measurable, it does not exist.

This, of course, is an incredibly narrow and limited view of all the possible ways of knowing. We cannot see love, time, or radio waves either but we know they exist. Instead of teaching our children the ways of honoring and connecting with Spirit, we have passed on a belief system that blocks and frustrates their deep inner yearning and leaves them incomplete and unprepared to face the challenges of life.

From the perspective of the philosophy of science, correct measurement must use tools that fit what is being measured. Observation through the physical senses and quantification must be on the same level as the phenomena being studied. Spirit, by definition, is not a sensory phenomenon and therefore not on the physical level. It is of a different nature and the measurement tools of quantitative science do not fit. They are inappropriate and irrelevant. Therefore, though we have properly accepted the scientific paradigm for understanding and manipulating the material world, to embrace it as a standard for gauging the voracity of Spirit is misplaced.

Buckminster Fuller, one of the creative geniuses of our century, said, "God is a verb not a noun." The divine mystery is not a being that does, it's an experience that *is*. It's our experience of the mountain top, the experience of a rainbow, the experience of the crashing waves, that is the proper proof of the truth of the God-force. The inner movement of wonder and awe is the evidence of the presence of the infinite Invisible.

If we understand the divine principle in this way, not as a super cop directing human traffic, but as a principle, an unknowable force that accounts for the law of gravity and the exquisite design of this body, then we can open to who we truly are, and enjoy the beauty which is our birth right.

Many people reject the existence of divine principle in reaction to the inequities and horrors that occur in this world. At bottom, this too stems from an anthropomorphic view of God. If there was a being in the heavens allowing the death of a child at the hands

of a mother, the abuse of a wife at the hands of a husband, geno-
cide, torture and all the unspeakable atrocities we humans inflict
upon each other, then surely that is not a God worth honoring. That,
however, is not the true nature of the God-force.

The cause of "man's inhumanity to man" is not a God gone mad,
nor a wrathful vengeful God. It is quite the opposite. The source of
our inhumanity is alienation from the divine. It is the lack of Spirit
at the center of our lives which makes it possible for us to reduce
our neighbors to our enemies. Those who truly hold Spirit in their
heart do not perpetrate horrors against others.

The first and most critical step in regaining inner balance is to
honor Spirit as the central element in our lives.

The "sacred" implies an encounter with the presence of Spirit.
In the spiritual metaphor of the Hebrew Bible, Yahweh speaks to
Moses saying, "The place upon which you stand is holy ground."
What inspiring words! Holiness dwells wherever you are, where you
stand, because it is within you. You are always in the presence of
the holy because you are a sacred being. As the Indian sage Sivananda
put it, "Just as rain exists in the clouds, butter in milk, fragrance in
flowers, so also God is hidden in all these names and forms."

We are all expressions of the divine principle manifest in human form. We are reflections of the infinite Perfection focused and
manifested into a being, into a human body. We individually are to
the divine principle as waves are to the sea. Each unique, individual
person is a singular wave, a reflection in limited form, of the vast
unified ocean of Spirit.

The ancient teachings of the Vedantic tradition, what we call
Hinduism today, describes this phenomena through the concepts of
Brahman and *atman*. The *Brahman* is the grand universal life force,
the God-principle in its vast form. The *atman* is the mirror image in
microcosm of this God-force dwelling within each of us. *Atman* is
the same energy as *Brahman*, manifested and constantly unfolding
within the individual person.

This pattern echoes the physical phenomena demonstrated by
cloning. Just as each cell in our body contains the whole structure
of our being, each individual soul reflects the divinity of the
Cosmos.

Jesus expressed this concept when he said, "I and the Father are one." The "Father" is a metaphor for the God-force. The Christ principle, manifested in Jesus, is the part within all of us which realizes our divine nature. Our eternal and constant oneness with God.

The God-principle within us is consciousness itself. The mirror of the vastness within us is not a physical structure in our bodies like a heart, or even a theoretical concept like a soul, but the actual element of consciousness which lies behind our humanness and defines us as living beings.

❋ ❋ ❋ ❋ ❋

EXCERCISE
To experience this yourself, put your attention on one part of your body, your nose for instance.

Now, become aware of what within you notices your nose. Turn your attention to a thought and recognize what notices the thought. Bring your awareness to a feeling. Then identify what notices the feeling. **It** *is consciousness itself*.

❋ ❋ ❋ ❋ ❋

This fundamental part of you, pure awareness, that which notices the noticing, is consciousness. It constitutes the ultimate indivisible aspect of who we are. Consciousness is the central organizing principle for all else.

What does your breathing for you? What translates light rays through your eyes into visual images in your mind? What courses your blood through your body? What is the essential life force? Pure consciousness itself.

Take note of the quality of the feeling you experienced when connected with pure consciousness. It has specific identifiable characteristics.

Most importantly, consciousness has the attribute of unity. There is no opposition, contradiction, separation, or conflict at the level of pure consciousness. There is a sense of spaciousness and peace. It is this unified ocean of consciousness from which the differentiated waves of experience arise. Consciousness is the *atman*. Consciousness is the inner seat of the Divine.

To avoid the pitfalls of anthropomorphism and cut directly to the experience of life force, Buddhists do not concern themselves with the idea of God. Rather, they focus on the practice of bare awareness, fully noticing every aspect of daily life, microscopically. From waking in the morning to sleeping at night, attention is fully focused on the bare activity. The movement of one's legs in walking, the action of our mouths in chewing, the exact sensation we experience when caught in traffic, and so on.

Because awareness is a pure reflection of consciousness, by fully focusing on it, dwelling in it, Buddhist practitioners bring forth Spirit in their moment-to-moment lives. Long practicing Buddhists are a model of serenity.

at whittington beach

standing on the shore
white waves pounding
unflinching rock

vast mother ocean
focusing into drops

we too are the Vastness
focused into beings

sea and spray
infinity and i
One

This is quite different from our habitual partial awareness where only a bit of our actual experience is noted while most of our attention is devoted to the thoughts passing through our minds. We would do well to learn from this ancient Eastern practice in order to realize the Western proverb, "The best way to make your dreams come true is to wake up."

Silence, Solitude, Stillness, and Simplicity

THERE ARE MANY OTHER doorways into the sacred. Numerous spiritual practices help recover Spirit in our lives. Most involve the elements of silence, solitude, stillness, and simplicity. Without the necessity for retreat to the hermitage, these practices serve to slow the churning mind, let it to come to rest at center, and allow our higher self, our Essence, to move from background to foreground. In silence, solitude, stillness, and simplicity we remember who we truly are and live more fully in balance. It is the methodology for what the poet Browning called, "Opening out a way for the imprisoned splendor to escape."

Silence and solitude create an atmosphere in which inner stillness grows. Most of the time the mind is busy processing the thoughts and details of our life. One helpful practice is to create Sabbaths and mini-Sabbaths in our lives. Times of rest within each day, days of rest within each week, and weeks of rest within each year. During your Sabbaths, become still and silent. Remove yourself from the outer bustle and reside in the inner stillness. During outwardly active days, your mini-Sabbaths may simply be a moment of turning inward for ten minutes with the door closed in silence.

Simplicity supports and allows silence to unfold. In a life filled with stimulation, the mind is often agitated. To bring forth Spirit, to dwell in Essence, it is helpful to spend time in environments where distracting objects are few.

Meditation is the most effective vehicle into Essence. It embraces and generates the qualities of silence, solitude, stillness and simplicity. It allows us to reside in a state of pure consciousness. Meditation, fundamentally, is simply quieting the mind. Once quiet, Essence naturally comes forward.

at wood valley

sitting on the Temple floor
it came clear

what we call "real"
is Illusion

what we call "illusion"
is Real

the Real world
is like an empty room
open and uncluttered

the wind blows through it
freely

Illusion
is a room filled with over stuffed chairs

in the emptiness truth is clear
freedom is natural
and happiness
is Real

There are numerous meditation techniques both classical and nontraditional. Most meditation is accomplished through focusing attention. Classical meditation practices generally involve focusing awareness on a single point of breath, sound, or sight.

Sound focused meditation is the repetition of a sacred sound often called a mantra. Chanting and repetitive prayer are also sound focused meditations. Mantra meditation may be the simple repetition in silence of the word "One," or an affirmation to one's self, "I am Essence." The affirmation method is particularly effective because it not only focuses the attention, thus unifying and quieting the mind, it also contains profound meaning reaffirming our true nature as the higher self.

Meditation on the breath involves noticing the movement of respiration as it comes in and goes out, either at the nostrils or the abdomen. In sight oriented meditation, the focus is unified by singularly attending to a visual cue, the eyes resting on an object or blank space. Both methods allow the thinking mind to come to rest.

During meditation, no matter what technique or focal point is used to unify attention, the mind will inevitably wander away to thoughts, feelings, or external stimuli. It is the nature of the mind to wander. The movement is perfectly normal and part of the overall meditation process.

When you are meditating by focusing on breathing, when you recognize that your mind has wandered to a thought, an external noise, or a feeling, without self-judgment or blame gently return the attention to the breath. All meditation has this dynamic quality of moving into and away from the center. Meditation is not about remaining at center, it is about returning to it.

Other activities that are not traditionally defined as meditation can serve the same function as classical meditation. Walking, running, swimming, all forms of active movement and sport, the arts, hobbies, gardening, or a single focused activity like painting a wall have an effect similar to sitting meditation. Like classical meditation techniques, they quiet the agitated mind, bring it to rest on a single focus, allowing the natural emergence of Essence.

It does not matter how we choose to meditate, but it is crucial to our balance and well-being that we do so.

The awakening of spirit reflects the dynamic pattern of the meditation process itself. It is a rhythm of forgetting and remembering. Remembering and forgetting. Remembering we are Essence, then forgetting again. Our attention wanders from remembering, and when we recognize that it has wandered, we gently return it to the awareness of our true identity as Essence. It matters little how often the mind wanders, it is the process of always bringing it back that is fundamental. If we are wise, we will remember to return often. As the Buddha said, "It does not matter how long we have forgotten, only how soon we remember."

The awakening of Spirit is fundamentally a process of self-identification. Shifting from the limited self-definition of a personality in a body, to a more expansive identification that recognizes our God-like qualities of *Brahman-atman*. The awakening of Spirit is the answer to the essential question, "Who am I?"

Am I this body? This mind? These feelings? When we step back from the "wheel of daily life," we know that we are more than any one of these aspects. We know that we are more than all three combined. But living in this physical world, getting lost in our day-to-day activities, we forget who we really are and take ourselves to be one of these limited aspects of self.

For example, when you are angry, if you closely examine your feelings, you will recognize that you are experiencing yourself not simply as *having* anger but actually as *being* anger. This is not unique to the feeling of anger, it holds true for any strong emotional state or constellation of thought.

If you are trying to choose between two difficult alternatives,

---

running

Adults at play
Childhood lives

The body in Movement
Long, fluid, graceful
Movement

Concentrated
Relaxed
Focused

Movement in Balance
the Dance

Lost
At One
running

and repeatedly bounce between the options, upon close self-examination you will notice that you do not just experience yourself as having confusion, you become confusion. That is why the discomfort is so powerful. Thus, constantly caught up in the experiences, thoughts and feelings of everyday life, we often identify with partial aspects of ourselves, forgetting our true identity as divine beings.

Properly understood, we *have* thoughts and feelings, but we *are* the higher Self. We have confusion and anger, but we are not confusion and anger. We are an integrated whole. We are Essence. We are spiritual beings with a mind, in a body, wrapped in feelings. The practices of silence, solitude, stillness, and simplicity through the vehicle of meditation will help us remember.

The harvest of nurturing Spirit is bountiful. In the Judeo- Christian tradition it is called "The peace that passeth understanding." It is the symmetry that comes when things are in their proper order. Recognizing, remembering, honoring and living in Spirit is in harmony with the essential order. The outflow of the inner harmony generates balance in the outer experiences of work, home and play.

A mind at peace makes better decisions, generates more effective action, and achieves better results than one in chaos. We move more skillfully and elegantly in the world, creating opportunities and reaping reward. It becomes easier to advance uninterrupted towards one's goals, with less effort and fewer diversions. It also profoundly and positively affects our health.

The revitalization of the spiritual life does not eliminate the hard parts. The pain, loss and grief of this mysterious process of living does not go away. Spiritual revitalization simply helps us remember and return to the ecstasy of Essence. As Albert Camus wrote, "In the middle of winter I found there was an invincible summer."

 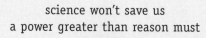

XXI

science won't save us
a power greater than reason must

science
in the end
is just a description
of the Creation

deeper
we must push
beyond thinking mind
to the Creation itself
to Spirit mind
to the Center

at the Center is the energy
to power the twenty first century

CHAPTER THREE

Love *and* Self-Acceptance

*Everything has to do
with loving and not loving.*
Jalal ad-din Rumi

L OVE IS THE FUNDAMENTAL energy of the Divine. When we identify with our Essence, we experience love. When we feel love, it
puts us in touch with our Essence. As the sixteenth-century
Christian mystic and reformer Martin Luther said, "Love is an
image of God, and not a lifeless image, but the living essence of
Divine nature."

The most important form of love is self-love. Self-love is fundamental to harmony within and balance without. When we love ourselves, we experience openness, peace and harmony. Others will bask
in the glow and reflect love back to us. Self-love manifests in our
outer lives as positive supportive experiences.

When we love and accept ourselves, we create a feeling of both
expansion and lightness of being. Like Jupiter, so expanded that the
eight other planets can rest comfortably inside its great mass, it is
also light, with a density only one-quarter of the earth's.

Without self-love, we are of little service to the world because without it we cannot truly love others. This is the case in our family, workplace, and community. A workshop participant said it well, after completing a stress training class that focused on meditation practice, "The more I love and accept myself, the more I love and accept those around me."

As a result of our puritanical heritage, there is a strong cultural bias against self-love. Instead, we emphasize self-criticism as the path to self-improvement. Many deem positive self-regard as arrogant. Even the sound of the two words together, "self" and "love" startles many people.

As a result of this unfortunate bias, we lack the ability to wholeheartedly love ourselves. In its place we emphasize the opposite, self-judgment and reproach. The inner experience of self-judgment, unlike that of love, is painful, damaging, and serves to alienate us from identifying with our higher Self.

The emphasis on self-criticism turns the injunction, "Love thy neighbor as thyself" into an empty platitude. We can not love our neighbor if we do not love ourself. If I don't love myself, then "loving my neighboring as myself" is no love at all. The result of our self-reproach is more likely hating our neighbor than loving him.

Self-judgment and -criticism may be the most harmful forces in our lives. The experience of self-judgment is harsh and painful. The actual process of self-criticism involves one element in our character condemning another. One part of ourself is determining that another is wrong, or out of line with our inner Judge's ideal. This process generates internal warfare because it sets ourself against ourself. Inevitably we project the inner conflict outward. It becomes anger, criticism or blame toward those closest to us. It gives rise to conflict at home, at work, and at play.

The most important ingredient in self-love is self-acceptance. Acceptance implies an open, receptive and welcoming attitude toward one's self. It means regarding ourselves as worthy exactly as we are, without any need for change or alteration.

How often do we hold this attitude toward ourselves? Do we even approve of such an attitude? It may be okay to consider someone else inherently worthy, a parent, a partner, or a child perhaps. But ourselves?

Instead of self-acceptance, our conditioned tendency is toward self-rejection. The natural overwhelming reaction to rejection is to feel hurt and close off to the source of the pain, thus fueling more inner battle. Rejection also produces the elemental painful emotions of fear, anger, and grief.

It is an immense challenge to overcome a lifetime of conditioning towards self-rejection. It takes great awareness and commitment to open to self-acceptance and its fruits. Self-acceptance facilitates the flow of self love and our natural connection with the divine bliss. As the great modern spiritual master of India, Ramana Maharshi said, "Man's real nature is happiness. Happiness is inborn in the true Self. Man's search for happiness is an unconscious search for his true Self. The true Self is imperishable; therefore, when man finds it, he finds a happiness which does not come to and end."

Psychotherapy and Self-Help

SOME OF THE institutions designed to help us on the journey to self fulfillment, like psychotherapy and the Self Help movement, are plagued with the cultural assumptions that generate self-criticism and ultimately self-hate. These assumptions are often unconscious or hidden, turning what is meant to be helpful into painful hindrance.

Most systems of psychotherapy practiced today are based upon a pathological model. The underlying assumption is that there is something wrong with the client and the broken part must be identified and fixed. For many therapists, this approach evolves into a surgical model; the pathology must be located and excised.

Even the best intentioned psychotherapists may be unaware of the assumptions underlying their work and the techniques they employ. As a consequence, therapists can unknowingly and unintentionally add to the client's burden by reinforcing the assumption that there is something wrong with them and sparking further self-reproach and inner conflict. Psychotherapeutic intervention can be like the Trojan horse. It appears as an ally but once inside becomes an antagonist.

The therapist's intention is invariably positive, but what can be communicated in the subtext is pathology and judgment. Being judged by someone in a position of authority stimulates powerful self-criticism in the patient. Inevitably, the underlying assumption of pathology is communicated to the patient in a subtle way through the language, questions, comments, and observations of the therapist.

A typical form of therapist-patient communication is "you would be fine if you didn't do x," or "the problem you have is in your y quality," or "if you were only to change toward z, things would improve." The patient then unconsciously or consciously has the inner response, "I'm definitely not okay the way I am, I have to be different." Self-criticism and inner conflict is heightened. The patient is less able to move toward a desired state because the energy necessary to do so is locked in inner discord, unable to release into the healthy unfolding of the new.

I was observing a group working with a psychotherapist recently and this process was strikingly obvious, yet unseen to the participants or the therapist. It gave me an uneasy feeling, like watching a magician whose trickery was obvious but invisible to the audience. In this case even the magician thought it was real. As the therapist worked with the group almost all her questions, asked with good intention, were statements of judgment in disguise. They were, "Bill, your such a strong man, why are you weak in the face of women ?" Or, "Jeanie, you could do that stuff with your eyes closed if you got over your fear around money." Like the Trojan horse, the appearance was support, the effect was defeat.

The self-help movement shares this assumption. The fundamental supposition of most self-help books, seminars and programs is that something is wrong with us and it needs fixing. It assumes we are missing something and they have what must be added. But there is the fundamental flaw in the arithmetic. It is not a matter of addition, but subtraction.

We are not missing anything. We may have forgotten our essential perfection, covered it with layers of illusion, but the job is not to add something from the outside. It is to uncover and release the perfection within. We are essentially whole beings evolving towards the discovery of our perfection.

The assumptions of self-help movement, like those of psychotherapy are imbedded and revealed in the language. "Your body is *too* fat, it needs to *get* thinner." "You are *too* fearful, you need to be *more* courageous." "You have problems with your parents, you *need* to get *over* them." "Your *not* high enough, you *need* to be *more* spiritual."

Of course, in offering this book I run the risk of creating self-criticism in the reader. My intention, however, is not to communicate that the way you are now is flawed. My message is that you are perfect. There is nothing to seek and nothing to find. There is only the remembrance of your divine identity and the honoring of all that you are. From there, the insights I offer are merely road signs on the journey.

The alternative to critically-based psychotherapy and self-help agendas is self care, which is fully accepting and loving and at the same time moving toward growth and change. Guidance that is supportive, positive and joyful, not judgmental or rejecting. That is the way of growth through self-love. It is more gentle, more pleasant and more effective.

My approach focuses on remembering who we really are and at the same time letting go of that which does not truly sustain us. It is the technique of *loving away the pain*. When we become aware that there is a part of ourselves that is not serving us, that an aspect within is causing pain, we do not have to respond with the conditioned reaction that this part must be criticized, rejected, or even eliminated. On the contrary, it is this aspect of ourselves which is experiencing a lack of love, calling out for attention. It needs soothing, embracing, and love. It needs completion so that it can release and ungrudgingly set us free.

It is as if the wounded parts of our personality call out for attention and care. It is the place of our higher Self to hear the call and respond with the healing force of love. A metaphor for understanding this relationship between our Essence and the wounded part of our personality, is the relationship between mother and child. When a little boy is hurting, he comes to his mother crying. He may have a skinned knee or hurt feelings. What attitude and behavior on the part of the mother is most effective? What attitude and behavior helps release the pain? If we reject the child and his pain, by invoking the cultural norm, "don't be a sissy, big boys don't cry," the child feels the physical pain more deeply and we add to it the emotional pain of rejection. As Mother Teresa said, "If you are judging someone, you don't have time to love them."

If we accept the child just as he or she is, in all their pain, receiving them openly and communicating to them their inherent value through our loving words and behavior, there is an immediate diminishment in the pain and the emotional support lifts their spirit. Acceptance in the face of adversity adds to the child's sense of self-worth built through the knowledge that she or he is loved.

A parallel process is at work within us. Our higher Self, our Essence is like the parent, our personality is like the child. If a part of the personality is in pain we don't reject it. Rather, like the wise mother we love it away. Opening to the part of the personality that is causing and experiencing difficulty, honoring it, receiving it as worthy and knowing that natural diminishment unfolds through this process of acceptance.

Examples of the effectiveness of change through love and the ineffectiveness of change through self-rejection abound. It is easily understood when we examine some of the most obvious areas in which we are self-critical. Our physical appearance. Our weight, for instance. Anyone who has been "overweight" knows, and much research demonstrates, that "diets don't work." (There is even a weight loss program by this very name).

Why don't diets work? Because the fundamental background assumption when one embarks on a diet is that we are not okay the way we are. We must change first and then we will be acceptable. The energy produced by the inner battle fuels the habitual eating routine. It's not that the diet itself doesn't work. What is prescribed to eat and not eat for almost all diets would almost certainly result in weight loss. It's the initial assumptions impelling us to diet that create the very dynamic that keeps us from actually executing it.

Examination of the inner process of obese people indicates that they are rejecting themselves in a much broader way than simply rejecting their body image. They begin in a globally self-critical state, take on the added self-criticism around the diet, the self-reproach each time they break it, until the struggle becomes overwhelming and they simply must give up. Then a binge ensues which is really a misplaced effort in self-love; a process aimed at self-comfort through eating. The sadness generated by this experience is profound and very touching.

Geneen Roth, author of *When Food is Love* and *Feeding the Hungry Heart* is one of the few practitioners to have success helping people lose weight. Her method is opposite to the pathologizing approach to weight loss via diets. She guides and supports her clients to find the place within that is self-rejecting. Identifying this source, is a necessary and sometimes sufficient component, in releasing the self-criticism. Roth encourages the client's full self acceptance, including the shape of their bodies just as they are, as well as their present eating habits. This helps to end their habitual inner warfare and allows the client freer access to energy which can support them in breaking out of the cycle of addictive eating and reproach. A large percentage of her clients return to the natural pattern of "eating when you're hungry and stopping when you're full," thus returning over time to their appropriate weight.

The other day I was working out in the gym and an interview program came on television. The theme of the show was obesity. The panelists were a number of men and women who were suffering from obesity along with their families. The panelists spoke of their lives, their problems and the bottomless sadness they felt from the effect their obesity had on their health and social relations. Their self-rejection was reflected back to them in rejection by others. Grief permeated the tone and you could feel it right through the television set.

One young person spoke of his rejection by his peers. Often, they didn't ask him to social events, "ditched" him when they became embarrassed of his looks, and made constant fun of his size. Another family—mother, father, daughter and son all obese—spoke of their fear that their father, the heaviest of all, would not live much longer because of the health problems associated with his weight. After his wife and children had shared these feelings, the father movingly spoke of his love for his family, his fear that he would lose them, and that they would be left without a father.

Spontaneously, the father stopped speaking and bowed his head in prayer. The others followed and, as appeared to be their custom, the father lead them in prayer. The words he meant to say were, "Dear God, please help us to lose this weight, it is a terrible burden to me and my family." Instead, what actually came out of his mouth was, "Dear God, please help me *love* this weight. . . ." Perhaps, as

Freud would suggest, his unconscious mind was pointing him in the right direction. A direction that might finally work to rid him of the dangerous weight, through self-love as an alternative to self-rejection.

An interesting and challenging paradox is that if we are to love and accept ourselves fully, we must love and accept even our self-rejection. It won't do to reject our rejecting self and accept our accepting self. The task is to receive and embrace even our rejecting self. Listen to it, honor it, understand it as a part of ourselves which for years has been trying to help us. Receive the rejecting aspect of ourselves until it is clear; this aspect is no longer serving to protect and improve. We can say good-bye and allow it to diminish on its own. Listen to the rejecting voice until it feels heard, then like the hurting child, being received and comforted, it can stop crying and rest.

An important exercise when we feel entrapped by a constricting quality within, is to drop into the Essence state, using the vehicles of quiet, solitude, and focus. From this condition, perspective and insight are accessible. Perspective allows us to see the big picture, the view from the mountain top, helping us honor all parts of ourselves, while at the same time remembering our fundamental identity as divine beings. Understanding that we *are not* this constricting quality, we *only have* this quality, and that we *are* Essence creates the space and courage not to judge but to allow.

Further, from the mountain top view of Essence, insight into the origins of the wounding which caused this constriction may arise. With the perspective of Essence, the causal level is more clear and accessible. Through the experience of insight, constriction gives way to release and a new level of equilibrium.

In Christianity the theme, "I and the Father are One," and the Hindu concepts of *Atman* and *Brahman* shout loudly and clearly, "You already are that which you seek." The places we wish to travel on our journey towards self-improvement, are places to which we have already arrived. What we are now, at this very moment, beneath the surface illusion that we are merely personalities in bodies, is complete wholeness. We need not wrestle with ourselves in order to be "better" people. We already are better people.

It is an interesting experience to sit with a spiritual Teacher, one who fully understands the truth of our own *a priori* perfection. He or she will speak in a church, a temple, a mosque or an auditorium and expand on the truth of this oneness. At the end of the talk, during the questions, almost every question asked continues to carry the assumption that we are imperfect, flawed, and how does the questioner fix that problem of self-pathology. "I am doing something wrong, what do I need to do to change it."

Invariably, the teacher patiently answers the question, touching lightly on the content of the specific problem presented, reminding the questioner in a new and yet different way that there is nothing to do or manipulate or change. Just, "be quiet and in tune with your higher Self, the clarity will emerge. Allow the perfection of who you truly are to emerge and disappear the problem for you."

Then, almost like we were playing roles in an absurd comedy, the next questioner asks the same thing in different words. "Such and such is wrong with me, it is painful, how can I change it." Again, patiently the teacher responds, lightly touching the subject matter and going on again to remind us of our Essence.

Outside the lecture hall, in life, this process seems to go on without end. It is a tribute to our teachers that they continue to listen and respond with love. It is a comment on our deep conditioning that it so hard for us to accept the truth that, "The place on which you stand is holy ground."

Developing the Capacity to Love

AS WE HAVE SEEN, the one unfailing way into self love is remembering our divine identity. When we remember our identity as divine beings, self-love naturally follows. Because love is the central quality of Essence, abiding in that state brings forth the experience of love in our life. When the 13th-century Sufi poet Jalal ad-din Rumi said, "Everything has to do with loving and not loving," he was also saying, everything has to do with remembering and forgetting.

To actually have an experience of this, notice the quality of the feeling within you when you identify with your Essence. Take a quiet moment and affirm, "I am Essence." Say it slowly, and open to its truth within you. Breathe it into your nostrils and let the knowing permeate your whole body. Now, notice how you feel. Do you experience the qualities of lightness, openness, and acceptance? You are in a state of love. Not the romantic love into which we "fall," but cosmic love into which we walk upright.

In this state we are already loving ourselves. Now, consider a part of yourself you have been rejecting. Imagine cradling it in the arms of Essence, gently rocking it into peace. Notice how, from identifying with Essence, it is possible to accept, even embrace, all aspects of our personality; and experience how those parts of ourselves then seem to quiet in the presence of love.

From Essence, we are also predisposed to loving others. The axiom, "we must love ourselves before we can love others," is not only logical but is a practical reality. If I am Essence, a microcosm of the divine, then of course you must be as well. Whatever difficult, distasteful or harmful behavior someone is manifesting in my presence, I can remember that underneath that conduct, at a deeper level hidden even to themselves, is their true Godlike nature. As the Christian teaching states, "We are all children of God."

It is possible to love others, even those we do not like, by the same process we love ourselves. Remembrance. Remembering who they truly are and relating to that higher Self rather than some unpleasant aspect of their personality and behavior. The reward is that "love given, is love received." Not only does it feel better to experience love in one's heart than disdain or hatred, when we feel it for others it is often returned to us. When we sense love we tend to respond back with love. Thus our remembrance of another's true identity serves to help them remember ours as well.

As the fundamental operative action in self-love is self-acceptance, the fundamental action which communicates love to others is also acceptance. Full unconditional acceptance of the other just as they are, with all their flaws. Acceptance without reservation and without precondition.

It is the feeling of being fully received and welcomed as worthy that communicates we are loved. Anything less and we know we are judged. When we sense even the smallest amount of judgment we feel diminished. We respond by defending ourselves against the aggression inherent in the judgment. Typically, we either close off or attack. Because closing and attack are not qualities associated with the higher Self, we have contributed through our judgment to moving the other person in the opposite direction of love.

Another approach to loving interaction with others is the capacity to substitute discernment for judgment. With judgment, we notice and reject. With discernment, we notice without rejecting. With discernment we maintain our ability to discriminate between what is constructive and destructive in another's behavior without closing our heart to them. Discernment is fully conscious and awake. It is noticing and choosing. Judgment is simply reactive, unconsciously pushing away.

We do not have to like someone to love them. We can see a quality in the other that we do not like, even feel strongly repulsed, and still keep our heart open through remembrance of their true identity.

With discernment we may choose to move away from a person we find distasteful, we may choose to speak our objection about the behavior that is disturbing. But still, at a deeper level, we honor the divinity in the other, even when it is not visible.

A puzzled disciple inquired with her Teacher about a difficult person in her life. She ran through all the options, expressed her confusion and finally, in exasperation asked the Teacher, "What shall I do?" The answer was as simple as it was true, "Do what you like with him, just don't throw him out of your heart."

This it is not an approach we have learned or are accustomed to using. We are conditioned to believe we must harden our hearts, close down or become aggressive in the presence of someone we do not like. The method of open heartedness even in the face of displeasure, though unfamiliar, is much easier on us and more helpful to the other. Not only does it feel better, it creates the conditions under which it is possible for the other to choose to change.

Similarly, unsolicited "helpful" advice is not helpful. Telling somebody what is wrong with them and how they can change, is rarely welcome and almost never effective. The underlying message in advice is that the person is not okay as they are and that they need to be different. It is an implicit rejection and creates a heart closing response.

We are all familiar with the difficulty and strain created within us when we try to change someone else. It is ineffectual and damaging. It's like trying to lift a thousand pounds without any mechanical advantage. You stress and strain but the weight does not move.

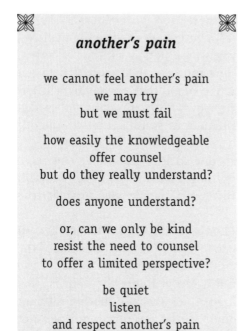

another's pain

we cannot feel another's pain
we may try
but we must fail

how easily the knowledgeable
offer counsel
but do they really understand?

does anyone understand?

or, can we only be kind
resist the need to counsel
to offer a limited perspective?

be quiet
listen
and respect another's pain

The only outcome is more pain.

The most effective and self-loving approach towards relating to those we don't like is to accept them as they are, without struggling to make them different. We thereby create the conditions under which they can choose to be different. We give them room to change. Magda Cregg said, writing about her partner the poet Lew Welch, "He made space around you so you could grow."

This, of course, is no magic bullet. Many people will not observably change at all. They aren't ready. They have many miles to travel and more work to do before any shift will emerge. But the experience of acceptance may serve as a help along the way. Like fruit that is unripe, it is not prepared to fall. It will not become sweet until it is ready, and it will not fall because we want it to. When it is time, under the right conditions, it will ripen and drop. Our acts of love and acceptance provide a bit more sunshine to speed the ripening process.

Listening as a Form of Love

THE BEHAVIOR that most effectively demonstrates acceptance and love is the simple but difficult act of listening. Listening without judgment or criticism. Simply receiving, receiving, receiving and more receiving. Listening fully is a love letter to the heart.

I worked for a training company many years ago that offered a program on listening to large corporate clients. The class was just one among many from which employees could choose. They generally enrolled in such courses to complete their necessary quota of training hours. Initially, to them, the listening course was just another class in the catalog, like spreadsheet skills or time management. Yet once the course began, slowly, over the course of two days, a very interesting shift evolved. The initial stiffness and distance began to melt. People relaxed, let their hair down, and dropped into a sense of comfort and safety. Employees who had been adversaries for years started connecting again. Smiles were growing dangerously wide. When we finished on the second day, we closed with time for each participant to share their experience of the seminar. There were many tearful eyes. Deep heartfelt sentiments were expressed. People shared how they hadn't felt so received and accepted for years. "Yes," one manager said, "I even felt loved." Such is the power of listening.

The curriculum for the listening training was designed around three basic principles whose acronym spelled AAA: "Allow," "Accept," "Acknowledge." These qualities, expressed as specific behaviors, constitute a good listener.

ALLOW the other person's communication to be just as it is, without any judgment, criticism, or need to change it.

ACCEPT their views as valid for them, even if they are not valid for you.

ACKNOWLEDGE what the other has said so as to clearly confirm that you have heard them. Behaviorally, acknowledgment means stating a simple account of what you understood. It might be something like, "I understand that you don't like people who push themselves into social situations. My own sense of it is . . . ." Acknowledgment is what makes it clear to the speaker that she has been received.

Many people resist fully giving themselves over to listening because they somehow believe, consciously or unconsciously, that listening implies agreement. If they do not agree with the content of the speakers words, they feel obliged to interrupt the speaker or focus their attention on constructing a response instead of fully listening.

Non-listening is often executed from the moral high ground with the conviction of a zealot. In fact, this style turns interpersonal communication, which can be deeply connecting, into something resembling a military campaign.

The non-listening, combative communication style is of course typical of argument. We state our point, the other is focused on constructing their attack or defense, we feel unheard, so we make our point more strongly. In the process we are not listening to the other. They feel unheard and raise their voice to make the point more strongly. The conflict escalates, the parties get more frustrated and angry, then rupture and disconnection ensue.

Our need to be understood is intense. We are willing to go to great lengths and endure great pain and conflict to be understood. When we do not feel heard, our natural response is to look for more powerful ways to make ourselves clear. Feeling we are not heard, we press on with greater force. Due to our lack of sophistication about effective communication, this generally means saying the same thing in a slightly different way, more loudly. In the process, we stop listening and communication deteriorates.

To break the cycle it is important to understand that listening is not agreeing with the speaker's content, it is honoring the speaker's person. This perspective is illustrated by the traditional East Indian greeting *Namaste*, "I honor the God within you."

If our views are at odds with the speaker's, the best approach is to first fully listen. By fully listening we have respected the speaker's truth and due to our close attention understand more fully their meaning. It is then our responsibility to make ourselves clear. Denying our own truth to give the appearance of agreement is not self-loving, it is just "making nice." To dishonor one's self in order to honor the other is not an acceptable alternative. Fortunately, it is not necessary. Honoring ourselves and the other are not mutually exclusive. We can fully listen and fully speak in the same interaction.

To respect our own beliefs, we do not need to prepare our response while the other is still talking. As we have seen, despite the urge to do so, preparation is non-listening and thus counterproductive. We only need to slow down enough to break the process into three steps, rather than rush it into one. (1) Listening fully; (2) considering our own response; (3) speaking. This method allows us to both respect the other and honor ourselves while disagreeing.

I was working with two business partners the other day whose communication pattern was predominately argument. No matter what the topic, they fought. From their body language it was clear that while one was speaking the other was digging in, devoting his energy not to listening and understanding but to identifying the weak points in the others' argument so he could blow holes in it at the first possible opportunity. There was no listening, just talking and preparation for talking.

During a break in the action, I pointed out this pattern to them. Surprisingly, they recognized it immediately. They agreed that they both came on too strong with each other and it was because neither felt heard. The argument, as they saw it, was not really a struggle to be right but a fight to be heard.

By way of coaching, I clarified the difference between listening and agreeing. I used the image of taking their own view off their lap and putting it by their side during the time the other was speaking. I reminded them to trust that their time would come, that in listening they would not be abandoning their view, but honoring themselves as well as the other. I said that by letting their position rest temporarily while the other spoke it would further the goal of better understanding their partner and communicating to the other that he has been heard. Then, when their partner was complete, they could pick up their own position, put it front and center, and explain themselves as vigorously and clearly as possible. This approach to listening is called "bracketing" by the psychiatrist and writer Scott Peck. He describes it beautifully in *The Road Less Traveled:*

> An essential part of true listening is the discipline of bracketing, the temporary giving up or setting aside of one's own prejudices, frames of reference and desires so as to experience as far as possible the speaker's world from the inside, stepping inside his or her shoes. This unification of speaker and listener is actually an extension and enlargement of ourselves, and new knowledge is always gained from this. Moreover, since true listening involves bracketing, a setting aside of the self it is also temporarily involves a total acceptance of the other. Sensing this acceptance, the speaker will feel less and less

vulnerable and more and more inclined to open up the inner recesses of his or her mind to the listener. As this happens, speaker and listener begin to appreciate each other more and more, and the duet dance of love is begun again.[1]

Because their intentions were positive and they shared the goal of maintaining a successful business, and because beneath their habitual argumentative communications style there was love and respect, with guidance the partners literally switched communication styles on the spot. Their interaction was transformed.

We returned to the issues that had been going in circles. This time both felt heard and understood, and the conflict around the content of the two topics faded away. They shifted into cooperative problem solving and quickly found straightforward solutions. When we finished they were elated. The business challenges were no longer worrisome and they felt individually more empowered. Further, they had invigorated a waning friendship.

The Nature of Blame

BLAME IS THE antithesis of love and the opposite of acceptance. Blame kills connection with self and other. The inner experience of blaming is dark and angry. It has none of the joyful quality of accepting.

Blame initiates a defensive reaction in the person blamed. In response, depending on their habits of personality, there is either attack or withdrawal. If the other withdraws, they are no longer available for further discussion and resolution. If attack is their conditioned form of defense, then the pattern is escalated further. This is what I call the "Cycle of Blame and Defense."

If the cycle is not broken by one party or the other having the presence to listen non-defensively, it can be very debilitating and harmful. The Cycle of Blame and Defense almost always ends in frustration and disconnection and a sense of disempowerment. It promotes the desperately frustrating feeling that we are in an inescapable bind and there is no way out. It can promote verbal abuse and in

---

1. M. Scott Peck, *The Road Less Traveled: A New Psychology of Love, Traditional Values, and Spiritual Growth* (New York: Touchstone, 1992).

some cases physical violence. In all cases, it heightens alienation from one's self and others.

Generally, we blame another as an alternative to experiencing a discomfort ourselves. An unpleasant circumstance or event arises, however trivial or big, and there is an immediate emotional reaction. In blame, as soon as the emotional body begins to feel annoyance, the mind races in to cast out the discomfort towards an external culprit. Because we are not accustomed to accepting our feelings and because we reject uncomfortable feelings as bad, we invoke unconscious mechanisms to remove ourselves from them. In the case of blame, we externalize the feeling, pushing it outside of ourselves onto another. If we can convince ourselves that the other has caused our discomfort, then we don't have to feel it ourselves. Furthermore, since the feeling associated with blame is most often anger, it allows us to stay in anger rather than experience the more difficult feelings of sadness or fear.

For example, it's time to go to work in the morning. I look for my keys on the table where I normally keep them, but they aren't there. Annoyance begins to arise, a subtle constriction in the body, frustration is emerging, fear associated with being late for work begins. Then, almost without conscious intention, a thought pops in; "Those kids were here playing with my daughter last night, they must have moved them." Then comes the shout, "Michelle where did those kids put my keys?" I have just initiated the unpleasant, unproductive and often relationship damaging Cycle of Blame and Defense.

Whether the circumstance is insignificant, like misplacing the car keys, or serious, as in a car crash, the event serves as a trigger for the fundamentally difficult feelings of fear and sadness. As an alternative we blame.

A more pernicious form of this dynamic is self-blame, When we do something that begins to generate fear or sadness within, as an alternative to deeply feeling that emotion, and in the absence of someone external to blame, we reproach ourselves. Self-blame is destructive because, as a more virulent form of judgment, it pits one part of ourselves against another. Over time we create a nagging internal enemy. It is as if we drop an antagonist commando behind our own lines to create chaos and disrupt harmonious functioning.

This inner self attack creates all the consequences of being under siege: injury, loss of confidence and self doubt.

Self-blame shifts the inner process from a strong emotional event, which left uninhibited and felt in the moment would pass quickly like a summer storm, into a long-lasting, crippling worry. It takes awareness and a measure of integrity to take the distasteful medicine of the short-term discomfort associated with feeling the feelings as they arise, in order to avoid the long-term debilitating effects of self-blame.

As much as I work on this issue myself, I see how profoundly conditioned I am to blame. I jump to it quickly, blaming myself and others before I am aware that it is happening. It is almost reflexive, so that sometimes the intervening moment for feeling the inner feeling does even seem to exist. I shift with lightning speed to blame in thought, speech, or action. If the coffee maker is in the wrong place my first thought is "why didn't she put it back where it belongs?" Then, I make a big fuss or try unsuccessfully to conceal my irritation. Until I remember that I took the coffee pot out to the studio and forgot to bring it back.

If I forget to bring home some papers from the office, I blame myself and move into self-criticism about my forgetfulness, which serves as an alternative to feeling the fear I have of giving my speech tomorrow without those well prepared notes.

The other day on the way down to Big Sur to give a workshop we stopped for gas in Monterey. I hopped out of the car, filled the tank, and we drove off. When we stopped for coffee ten minutes later I noticed that I had forgotten to put the gas cap back on. Harsh self-blame arose immediately. "I hate being so sloppy," I said to myself, "I just hate it."

I took this event as an opportunity to learn something about my blame and self-blame. I returned to the initial feeling I had experienced when I realized I lost the gas cap, and I knew underneath the anger was sadness and fear. When I stayed with the feelings, associations from childhood came to me. I remembered times when I forgot or lost things and got into deep trouble for it. Specific images arose of the time I forgot my bicycle at the school yard and it was gone when I returned to pick it up. My mother was incensed by that and her fury scared the hell out of me. I saw the time I lost a new jacket and got screamed at for it.

The reward for not blaming myself and staying with the feelings was that the wounded pattern that unconsciously arises whenever I lose or misplace something became conscious and amenable to healing. I understood that it is old pain that I am experiencing, not a response rooted in the present. It is becoming more clear that when I fall into self-blame, I lose an opportunity to continue deconditioning myself and be free to respond appropriately in the moment.

The Cycle of Blame and Defense is endemic to organizational life. All of us who have worked in organizations know this and have been on all sides of the blame experience. If the business didn't get a contract then "whose fault is it?" "It's the Bidding section's fault for not coming in low enough." The Bidding section blames Accounting, "It's the Accounting department's fault. They didn't provide the right numbers." The Accounting department blames Administrative Services, "We never get the manpower we need from Administration to take care of these rush jobs." Of course the waterfall of blame only serves to avoid feelings and cover our ass. It does nothing to help organizational effectiveness or improve profitability.

The Cycle of Blame and Defense is common at the community and national level also. When there is a communal problem, particularly in the case of disasters, placing blame is our first order of business after handling the crisis. Any event that generates a high level of fear or sadness will immediately generate a cycle of blame and defense in order to externalize the feelings. This usually generates anger instead of fear and grief.

The energy that would otherwise have to be felt is directed towards finding a culprit. Once found, culprit number one will pass it on to culprit number two, and so on. It's a bit like the children's' game "hide 'n seek." Everyone hides and whoever is unlucky enough to be chosen as "it" must then find and tag someone else as "it." In the case of community and national level events we empower the media to play the hide 'n seek game for us.

The primary emotional experiences of grief and fear that are stimulated by disasters go unexperienced. When the true feelings are denied, and the anger is misplaced, the outcome is seldom healing and sometimes absurd. For example, when there is a devastating fire and the community blames the fire department. A series of rapes and people blame the police department. The very men and women most active in solving these problems and most likely to risk life and limb to do so are blamed because of our lack of courage to feel our own fear.

This happened in our small community a few years back. There was a fire, begun by children playing with matches, that turned into a disaster for the forest and the homes nestled in and around it. For months, even years, afterwards, the letters to the editor section of the local paper was filled with recrimination and blame. Everyone blamed a different and sometimes opposite entity. "Blame the children." "No, it wasn't the children's' fault." "Blame their parents." "No, it wasn't the parents' fault." "Blame the fire department." "No, it wasn't the fire department's fault." "Blame the county." "No, it wasn't the county fault." Blame the state, blame the federal government, blame the. . . .

National Public Radio ran a story on the number of vacant seats open on our national regulatory boards, such as the Federal Transportation Association, and Federal Housing Authority. The anchor switched to a reporter in the field covering the story. Her first words, designed to capture the public's attention were, "Who is to blame for this." She went on to say that Congress claims the President is "to blame." She interviewed Congressmen who spent their air time "blaming" the president. They switched to a White House spokesperson who whined Congress is "to blame." This is standard form for most media stories. Little analysis, little insight. In the place of analysis and insight, we are provided heaping servings of blame.

The Cycle of Blame and Defense is deeply imbedded in our thinking. It is so buried, that we seldom know we are in it. As these news stories illustrate, it is our natural and unexamined way of facing, or rather not facing, difficulty.

Tragically, blame gets us nowhere. It gets me nowhere when I blame my daughter or her friends. I don't find my keys any faster and I don't learn anything about myself. It gets me nowhere when I blame Barbara for something she may or may not have done. It really doesn't serve business organizations to blame the Marketing Department or the Accounting Department for the loss of a contract. A true look inside will produce more insight about where responsibility lies and where improvement is possible.

It doesn't serve our communities and nation either. Our habitual style of public debate, resembling little more than a badminton match with blame as the birdie, needs to change. We need to look inside, experiencing and understanding our problems at the real causal level in order to develop solutions that serve us.

I watched the American 100-meter relay team in the World Championship in Athens. There was tremendous pressure for them to succeed. Americans are supposed to be the fastest sprint team in the world, but lately, for one reason or another, they have been losing in the big international competitions. After an enormous media buildup, they did not even qualify for the finals. The baton was dropped during one of the earlier rounds and they were disqualified. The immediate media response was massive blame. The coaches were to blame, the athletes were to blame, the national federation of track and field was to blame. All a distraction to experiencing the disappointment.

And the athletes response, the individuals who had actually suffered the disappointment?. Blame and accusation? No. They united in their sadness. Pushed nothing out at others, just supported each other, committing to doing better next time. It was a very beautiful, very instructive lesson in alternatives to blame. The participants grew from their sadness and as some of them said, it was a more valuable experience than any gold medal could have ever been.

Feeling accepted and loved by others, facilitates our loving and accepting ourselves. If you can love me and accept me after I have made a mistake or failed, then surely I can love myself. When a child feels love from her parents, she tends to feel positively towards herself. The process is the same in adult relationships. When we feel loved by our partners, friends, or work mates we feel loving toward ourselves. We are able to grow in self love through the experience of being loved by others.

I have been in relationships where I didn't feel loved. During those times I didn't feel good about myself. I felt stagnant and uncreative. When things changed and I was in a loving relationship, I came much more into my power and potential. I had the courage born of self-love to explore areas that were risky but exciting and fulfilling. In the end, these explorations produced great rewards.

Some might say, "That's all very well for developing self esteem.

But how do we actually change things? Don't we have to find who made the mistake and fix blame so that it won't happen again?" My answer is a resounding, "No." If we look at what makes effective change, it is not fear induced or blame induced or a result of criticism. Change comes through the confidence engendered by love.

The mind-set that error must be punished through criticism in order to generate improvement is fallacious and pernicious. We do not need reproach to improve. Accountability and responsibility are definitely necessary and very useful. But criticism and blame are not. Guidance and feedback in the context of acceptance works much better. Loving support in the face of error is more effective for improving future performance then the crippling impact of blame.

When do you perform better, when the boss comes down on you for making a mistake and looks over your shoulder until you get it right? Or when she points out the error and supports you in finding ways to change and improve?

If the fire department really did screw up, how can we support them to do a better job? If the children did start the fire, how can we help them make amends?

Think of a time when you "did something wrong." How did you respond to those who blamed you? How did you respond to those who loved and accepted you right through it? Which helped more in improving your ability not to make that error again?

Standing for Yourself

THE JUDEO-CHRISTIAN tradition and some orthodox eastern religions teach us to sacrifice ourselves for the sake of others. We seldom do, of course, but we believe we should. It is deeply ingrained.

The origin of this directive lies in the belief that selflessness in regard to the small self, the personality, raises one's consciousness to a higher plane. As in meditation, when the small self recedes, the higher Self comes forward.

Sacrificing ourselves for another may be appropriate on rare occasions when heroic action is demanded or dire consequences may ensue. In most cases, however, putting others before ourselves becomes a rationalization for not taking good care of ourselves. It becomes a philosophy which helps us evade the very difficult work of standing for ourselves and loving ourselves enough to do what we need.

The most important object of our love is ourselves. The needs of our small self, our personality, are not to be diminished because we are awakening to our larger identity as Essence. Like the child with all his ignorance and faults he desperately needs to be loved and accepted. If we only give to others at the expense of ourselves, it is rather like a parent giving only to the wife and not the children. How would they feel? Unimportant, unworthy, left out, cold, sad, and angry.

The emotional component of our own personality must be nurtured. It must be loved. One of the most important ways it knows it is loved is through acceptance, non-criticism, non- judgment, and an open receiving attitude. Considering one's self as worthy, as primary and deserving to be put first, is essential. Just as it is central to the healthy development of children that they feel they are first in their parents eyes, it is fundamental to healthy adult personality development that we be put ourselves first as well.

i gave an old man
a hand
at Union Square
and it made me feel good

so i tried it again
across the street
from Grace Cathedral

until
he pushed a board
with a nail
in my face and said
"beat it
sucker,
forever"

We must take care of ourselves. Stand for ourselves. Communicate from Essence to our personality, "I am there for you. I will not abandon or forsake you." The values propagated by orthodox religion are an indication of traditional religions lack of sophistication and understanding about individual psychology and the integration of the emotional and spiritual life. Many people, in an effort to live up to spiritual injunctions, diminish themselves and their own needs. It is like the instance where we tell the little boy not to cry because he should be manly. We hold forth some supposedly higher value as an objective and deny in the process the real experience of the child. Denying the need to love and nurture our own personality is treating ourselves as if we deserve only second best.

It's unhealthy and counter productive for religious imperatives to diminish the fundamental need to stand for and love ourselves first, so that we may be capable of loving others.

At the moment, I am in a dispute with an organizational consultant. He and I have worked on a number of projects together when I needed extra help. Before I began a recent project, I requested his perspective to broaden my own. We had coffee together and talked about it for an hour. Later, when the project was completed he demanded half the fee.

I offered to pay him for the hours he consulted with me but that didn't satisfy him. He wanted half of the total fee claiming we were partners on the project. When I refused and explained that we were not, he became very angry and threatened to sue. I made a continued effort to resolve the matter cooperatively, but he wouldn't talk it through.

So, I defined a limit in support of myself and refused his continued verbal abuse. He is now proceeding to sue me in Small Claims Court.

There are certainly things I could have done better in this matter. I could have communicated more clearly and done a better job of clarifying our relationship on this particular project. However, his reaction was very aggressive and his communication definitely abusive. To accede to his eventual demands would have been to abandon myself in order to avoid the friction.

The conflict has been disturbing. I noticed a strong emotional reaction at each step in this unpleasant process. The strategy of "turning the other cheek," has called to me often. It is appealing as it is bathed in the moral high ground of religious teaching. On reflection, however, I see that I cannot turn the other cheek because to do so would really be just an excuse to avoid the situation. It would allow one part of myself to minimize discomfort by throwing another to the wolves. I must take care of my whole self. I must say no to his offense. I must create a limit beyond which he cannot cross as an act of self-love.

I have learned a lot from this difficult professional interaction.

In the past I often capitulated to aggressive people like the consultant, and ultimately felt diminished in the process. By standing for myself, I have stayed with the difficult feelings and received a great deal of insight into the roots of my previous self-abandonment.

When I was a boy my mother often verbally, and sometimes physically, abused me. Not terribly or horribly so, not constantly, but occasionally. Most of the time she was an extremely loving good hearted woman and I cherish her memory. Still, regardless of her overall demeanor, and despite the fact that her abusive behavior originated in her own father's abuse, her fits of temper and volcanic anger were devastating to me as a child. When frustrated and angry, she "lost it" and took after me with harsh words and a leather belt. When I defended myself, she became more enraged. I learned then that the best way to survive these episodes was to be passive and take it.

The scenarios would begin when I did something "wrong," as a children often do. Depending on my mother's mood, she might respond completely out of proportion to the offense. If I defended myself, it lead to "the strap."

I developed a survival strategy of not defending myself, which was inappropriate and devastating to me later in life. I had a number of violent confrontations in my youth in which I went into conditioned nondefense and got my ass kicked. The conditioning was so strong that the shut down response came forward before the normal biologically programmed fight or flight response set in. That unconscious patterning, which reflexively came out under attack, not only resulted in physical injury but was devastating to my sense of self-worth.

With the consultant incident, I have a new opportunity to dismantle this old pattern and shape a better one. I have the chance now to stand for myself in an act of self-love. I will not turn the other cheek. I will fight the law suit and do what is necessary to make it crystal clear that I will no longer "take it" as a form of self-defense and self-love.

Interestingly, as I stand for myself, the desire for adolescent revenge is not present. Before, in these kinds of situations, when I have capitulated, my feelings wavered between passive and aggressive fantasies; appease the aggressor or cause him harm. Now, I notice by taking care of myself, loving myself, standing for myself, I do not feel moved toward either the passive or aggressive response, but stand solidly in the loving one.

Authenticity

A MEASURE OF the extent to which we love ourselves is our authenticity. Being authentic is honoring who we are at the levels of higher Self and personality. Authenticity is loving ourselves enough to be true to who we are, unwilling to pose in order to satisfy the expectation of others or win their approval.

affectation

affectation
makes beautiful women ugly

smart men stupid

and everybody less

Authenticity is being genuine, natural, and real. When we are phony, dissemble, or put on false faces for interpersonal or material gain, we diminish ourselves. Inauthenticity is like the mother who leaves her child uncared for in exchange for the buzz of a hot date.

Authenticity is a rare quality. Like a diamond, its rarity is one of the reasons it commands so much respect. The pressure to be accepted drives us to limit our behavior within narrowly prescribed normative limits. From a cultural perspective, norms serve the function of keeping social institutions running smoothly. The rules are designed to minimize uncertainty, and if we conform to them we are rewarded. If we diverge we may not get the goodies all good little boys and girls get for being restrained.

What if our inner guidance does not move us in the same direction as the mainstream? What if we hear a different drummer? Do we love ourselves enough to march to it? Do we have the courage to decline the goodies and choose for ourselves?

The more homogeneous and intact the culture the stronger its control over us. Traditional societies have very strong normative systems and strong enforcement mechanisms, forcefully demanding its constituents to conform. The romanticization of traditional cultures like the Native American, Aboriginal, or Maori is due to our longing for authenticity, belonging, and community. The truth is, in these rigid types of social structures there is little room for following one's own star if it differs from the standard star map promoted by the mainstream.

I grew up in Detroit during the 1950s in a Jewish neighborhood and subculture. Acceptable and unacceptable behavior were clearly and narrowly defined. I hated it. I felt squashed by its rigidity, unable to express my natural self without suffering recriminations. When I faked it, acted the good little boy, I was rewarded. When I played the game by someone else's rules, I was a winner. But when I followed my own guidance, I was often the outsider.

I was ecstatic the first day I went off to university. Leaving the house and neighborhood, moving into a dorm room with someone I didn't know from a different culture, away from home in a college town, I soared. I explored myself, became more fully alive, even though there was a price to pay. I wasn't disappointed. The heady joy of authenticity was intoxicating. A reward far more gratifying than the social approval accompanying conformity.

After college, when I moved to California, the exultation expanded. Now, I was in an atmosphere that was not just absent of narrow limits but positively supported the true expression of self. Whatever its faults, the California of the 1960s supported the expression of authenticity.

Inauthenticity is a short-run fix and a long-run blunder. The price is inescapable and high. It is the cost of not loving ourselves. It is the cost of waking up in the middle of the night, with the devastating realization: "What have I done with my life? I wanted reds and blues but I chose all gray."

Authenticity demands honesty with ourselves and truth with others. It is loving ourselves more than caring what other people think. It is never too late for that.

CHAPTER FOUR

Heart Work

*Listen my friend, this road is the heart opening . . . . The heat of
midnight tears will bring you to God.*
Mirabai

OUR CULTURE IS BIASED AGAINST deep feeling. Those who feel
are somehow less than those who think. The pervasive belief
is: no matter how heavy your heart, ignore it, and put on a happy
face. If you do so, you will be rewarded. If you feel your feelings,
you will suffer for it.

We suppress and deny our emotions even more than we do our
spiritual nature. As mistaken as most organized religions are on the
true character of Spirit, believers at least acknowledge spirituality
as being at the core of their lives. But emotion, as seen through the
dominant male cultural perspective, is unseemly and a sign of weakness. Therefore, it is rejected. Rejecting a fundamental defining characteristic of who we are, our humanness, is one of the major reasons
for the lack of harmony in our lives.

It is like the person who disapproves of some physical feature they have and rejects it through hiding or pretending it's not
there. The part doesn't go away, we just pay an additional price by
denying it. When a person with crooked teeth smiles, always keep-

ing their teeth hidden behind closed lips, they look unnatural. When we act as if we don't have the feelings we so obviously do, we engage in the same inauthenticity.

Besides being as central and natural to us as our eyes or ears, emotions are an essential resource for living our lives in fullness and balance. Emotions are the doorway to critical information about our needs that reside below the level of our awareness. Our conscious mind has access to only a limited repository of information. Underneath, in what I call the "not yet conscious," is a vast storehouse of knowledge. Access to this information is central to making the inner shifts which result in dynamic balance.

The logical mind is dualistic, for every thought there is the tendency toward an equal and often opposite thought. Because the moral and social censoring mechanism of the mind is so strong, some ideas are judged unacceptable. For this reason, the logical faculty alone does not provide sufficient guidance to make sound decisions.

> ### *natural man*
>
> non-denial of what is
>
> clean
> simple
> sharp
>
> painful too
>
> nothing is owed
> no one is owned
>
> everything is connected
>
> honestly
> courageously
> free
>
> natural man.
> non-denial of what is

For example, I may be attracted to a female colleague. But my internal moral and ethical system says that this is not acceptable. Therefore, I deny that the feeling of attraction is there. In this high minded process, using the moral censor, I lie to myself. I do not allow myself to see the truth of what actually is, whether I like it or not.

Through the process of denial, I leave myself in the vulnerable position of being unaware of what is true for me, yet still under its influence. This is a dangerous situation because I cannot effectively act if I don't know the true status of my situation. I cannot reject an option that I do not allow myself to know is there. The hidden energy of the attraction creates its own dynamic and drives the situation into chaos. In contrast, opening to the truth of my feelings, knowing the attraction is there and the complications it might present, allows me to choose my behavior more gracefully.

If we learn to use our emotional assets, we can access information from the not-yet-conscious, a resource that presents information to us in a clear non-dualistic manner. The material is transparent without contradicting opposites. It is not limited by the self-censorship that creates a maze of shoulds and shouldn'ts. We then have enhanced internal guidance as well as access to data that is more reliable for us in the moment. Our decisions and actions become more appropriate to our here and now and produce results that create balance.

In denying our emotions, we are a ship without a compass. We leave ourselves without the necessary information to safely plot our course through the sometimes treacherous waters of everyday life.

Every society differs in the amount of emphasis they place on the importance of each of the four elements of the self; body, mind, emotions and Spirit. Our culture puts emphasis on body and mind. We increasingly honor the body in both negative and positive ways. The power of mind is almost worshipped.

It is not the same the world over. In the India, Spirit is revered. Latin cultures recognize and respect the centrality of emotions more than most. No society or nation that I know of integrates all four elements of the self. In this sense, the entire human family shares our imbalance.

More fundamental than the cultural taboo in our society against feeling our feelings, is the barrier to emotional work presented by the universal human tendency to cling to the pleasant and push away the unpleasant. Experiencing our emotions in their fullness means allowing both highs and lows their place. Emotions are as often unpleasant as they are pleasant. Of the four basic categories of feelings—anger fear, sadness and joy—three are difficult.

Because of our natural pattern, if the emotion is not joy, we tend to reflexively pull away from it. Anger, sadness and fear are feelings we would rather avoid than examine.

In opening only to emotions that we are attracted to and rejecting the others, we sacrifice an important internal feedback mechanism that allows us to recover harmony. I see this pattern in myself every day. For example, in the morning, I frequently select a card from a Tarot deck sitting on my dresser. Tarot cards are a teaching device originating in the Hebrew and Egyptian traditions. Each card has different words and symbols on its face. You select a card or cards randomly with the deck face down so you can't see the card you draw until you turn it over. The traditional purpose of the Tarot is divination.

I use the cards differently. I employ them as projective tools to clarify for me what is below the surface the way psychologists and psychiatrists use ink blotter tests with clients. Because the symbols and words are non-specific and open to a wide variety of interpretation, one can project into them one's own meaning. This process brings to the surface the material lying just below our present field of consciousness. Rather than assuming a fixed meaning for each card, they become a screen upon which the not yet conscious comes to life. This projecting process mimics the action and outcome of "feeling the feelings/emotional release work" described in Chapter 5.

When I draw a card whose symbols are unpleasant, I have the reflexive urge to deny it, put it back in the deck as if it never appeared, and pull another until I get one I like. Conversely, if I draw a card that makes me happy, I am satisfied and ready to go. Two days ago, I drew a card that said, "Stagnation" and before I consciously thought about it, I grabbed for another. Yesterday, I drew one that said "Sorrow" and I was immediately ready to put it back, as if the universe had made a mistake in this one case. Today, I drew a card that said "Illumination" and I was happy, leaving it in plain sight for everyone in the house to see.

However, two days ago, when I allowed myself to go inside and examine my projections around the card and word "Sorrow, " clarity emerged about a lingering sense of dissatisfaction I had been feeling for some time. I saw the previously hidden and suppressed sense of sorrow I was feeling about my daughter having left for college.

Though it was hard, I let myself feel how much I really missed her. The tears flowed. Through opening myself up to that sorrow, and feeling it, the sadness gradually dissipated. I felt more clear, happy for her, happy for me, and able to be in the moment.

Similarly, the next day when I examined the "Stagnation" card, I could see that I had also been repressing a sense of boredom that was present too often. I was feeling stagnant, but since it's such an unpleasant feeling I chose to deny it, talk myself out of it and pretend it wasn't true. I told myself stories like, "You can't be bored, life is too interesting. Every moment is precious. All you need to do is stay in the present and it's always interesting. There is no such thing as boredom," and so on.

Though these statements may be true, my real experience in time and space was of stagnation. In the long run, it is impossible to successfully repress the truth of one's inner experience, no matter how good the story. If the feeling is there, repression will only hide it, not take it away.

Once I allowed myself to be aware of the stagnation and opened to how it actually felt—definitely not a pleasant experience—the payoff was big. I saw clearly that I had not been devoting the time to my creative work that I need to do to feel good about myself. When I allowed myself to feel the stagnation, I knew with a certainty that my love for the creative process would overcome the block that I had been experiencing. Soon I was back in the saddle, writing away.

The unpleasant feelings are often more helpful than the pleasant ones. They are windows to our hidden inner process and allow us to better understand the truth of our experience. By wrestling with our negative feelings, we give ourselves the opportunity to dismantle the road blocks that our suppressed feelings become. This allows the natural process of growth to come forward.

The nature of our constantly evolving growth is to experience ourselves more and more as our higher Self. Staying awake to all our feelings, good and bad, high and low, we help ourselves move gracefully and speedily forward. If we reject some of our feelings because their initial bite is unpleasant, we run the risk of long-term difficulties.

The policing of our difficult feelings is not only internal, it is enforced by our friends and neighbors. It's not right to feel down. It is better to feel up. We get this message in many different ways. "Quit your whining" "Why are you so down?" "Quit worrying, everything will be okay." "It's nothing." "Don't sweat it." And, best of all, "Please don't cry." Feeling difficult emotions is not what our culture supports or rewards. It as though we have all agreed to suppress our pain.

I was in my twenties during the late sixties. Authenticity was emphasized, but there was and even stronger norm to "stay high." That didn't mean be stoned all the time. It meant that a real flower child was a happy flower child. This counterculture conformity left me alienated from many of my friends. I was struggling through the process of developing self-identity, and it wasn't easy or happy. Central to this process is an encounter with the dark side. Volcanic eruptions were arising within me every few days. They weren't pleasant, but they were real and they were mine, and they became allies on my journey toward wholeness. The pain I was feeling was exacerbated by my friends because of their ridicule of my being "down." The implication was that there was something wrong with me. I shouldn't be having those feelings; I should be enjoying the beauty of life.

Of course, life is infinitely beautiful. But feeling the full range of one's feelings is beautiful, too. There is beauty in night as well as day, moon as well as sun. There is pain and pleasure, down and up. It is more in tune with the beauty of the creation to open to all of it, feel all of it, and experience the wholeness than to pick and choose from the narrow range the majority defines as acceptable.

Nothing is a better indicator of our sentiment about difficult feelings than our social reaction to crying. Crying is not honored for its fundamental importance in maintaining our well being. Tears are nature's internal shower. Crying is the way in which emotional pain is transferred from inside to outside and released. Yet, there is a strong taboo against crying. Most of us have learned this lesson well and suppress our tears as if it were the correct and appropriate behavior.

It's a crock. A total tragedy. The suppression of our tears is unhealthy. We keep ourselves in pain because of our unwillingness to experience the process that will release it. The measure of how well our society re-integrates emotion as a fundamental part of our humanity will be the extent to which crying becomes an honored and accepted behavior.

I teach a graduate school course in Advanced Group Facilitation that focuses on depth work in the group setting. Students learn how to help and support clients through the emotional barriers that are inhibiting them. To do this, students must become familiar with emotional release work in their own lives. Much our our time is spent encouraging students to overcome the barriers to feeling their feelings and working with their own emotions and the healing insights that arise.

Recently, I ran into a former student who came from a country where the expression of feelings is frowned upon She had a difficult time with the class, but to her credit she took an experimental attitude and made huge gains in her personal growth and professional skills. When we met she said to me, "That class really changed my life. As you say in California, 'it transformed me.' I see things more clearly and experience things more fully. Most of all I feel more light and real. The biggest change, the one that has made the biggest difference in my life, is that I learned to let myself cry."

The denial of feelings is prominent both in the family setting and the work place. This is particularly true during times of interpersonal conflict. Much of my consulting practice involves conflict resolution work. After the individuals or groups involved tell their story about the conflict, I often ask the dreaded question, "How do you feel about all this." The most common reply is, "I think such and such," further describing their thoughts about the problem and their view of its causes. I might reply, "I understand your analysis of the problem, I have a pretty good grasp of what you think, but how do you feel, right now in this moment?" Amazingly, the most common response is, "Well, I think such and such..." The capacity to feel, to understand that a feeling is occurring and that it too has meaning, appears to be almost absent in many of us. It is as if we are emotionally illiterate.

I was working with two machinists in a client organization who were in a state of such intense conflict that little work was getting done. Their body language and tone of voice clearly revealed that they were tied up in emotional knots. When I brought them together to work on resolution, they would scream at each other, blame each other, and call each other nasty names. Yet when I asked, "What are you angry about?" they would both quickly say, "I'm not angry," denying any such feeling. "I'm not angry," they would shout, "I just think he's a son of a bitch," failing even to recognize the obvious humor in their emotional blindness. Despite the fact that emotion was the central feature of their experience, it wasn't okay to have a feeling, so they rejected it. They seemed to believe that if emotion was present they were diminished. Both were eventually fired by their boss because they could not get the work done with all that non-existent emotion in the way.

Sadly, the problem between these two men was not even a difficult one to solve. If they had been willing to drop to the level of feelings, where it could be resolved, the conflict would have had a happier ending. I knew that Bill was angry because Dan was using his tools. Dan was accustomed to the practice of sharing tools in other shops he had worked in and considered it normal procedure. Bill felt disrespected by Dan's attitude toward his private stuff but never spoke to Dan directly about it. Dan, on the other hand, was angry because he felt he was constantly getting a cold shoulder and 'bad vibes" for no apparent reason. The quality of his work was not recognized, and all he heard from Bill was criticism.

From my experience in similar conflicts, I knew that all that was needed was for each to express their anger (and sadness) at not getting the respect each felt they deserved. Then, it would not have been difficult to find a solution about the surface issue of tools. Instead, as a result of their lack of communication and denial of feelings, they both lost their jobs.

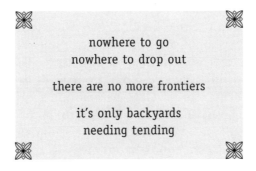

nowhere to go
nowhere to drop out

there are no more frontiers

it's only backyards
needing tending

CHAPTER FIVE

Emotional Release Work

Let my hidden weeping arise and blossom.
Rainer Maria Rikle

WITH OUR EMPHASIS ON body and mind, Americans are less skillful in understanding and dealing with Spirit and emotion. We need
to learn some fundamental skills in order to regain our natural balance. Let's begin by seeing Spirit and emotions as two halves of a
circle. Using the Taoist yin yang symbol—a circle with a curved line
dividing a dark half from a light half—we can represent Spirit on
one side and emotions on the other.

To come into internal harmony we need to develop both sides
of the circle. Developing the spiritual side means realizing our spiritual nature. As discussed in Chapter Two, through the use of silence,
solitude, and meditation we remind ourselves and remember our
identify as Essence. To develop the emotional half, for most of us
the darker side, requires some new definitions and skills.

Up to this point, I have used the terms "emotion" and "feeling"
interchangeably, a convention in our language. There is a difference

between the two words not generally recognized even in dictionaries. Emotions and feelings are at different levels of generality. The experience of each is distinct. Feelings, as the literal word implies, are specific physical sensations in the body. Emotions are a constellation of feelings that taken together, we subjectively experience and define as a generalized state. A feeling is, for example, a sensation of tightness in the stomach, or pressure in the temples, or trembling in the hands. These feelings, taken together, we might call the emotion of anxiety.

The confusion is exacerbated because the two words are often used in the same phrase, with feeling as the verb and emotion as the noun. For example, "I am feeling anxious this morning." What does this actually mean? The feeling, or physical sensation, is not actually anxiety, because there is no such physical feeling. Usually, the physical feelings in the body associated with our emotions are not concretely experienced because we are focused on the generalized mental level, constructing meaning, rather than sensing the body itself.

If we drop below the level of meaning, to what we actually experience, the specific physical sensations in the body, then we are in touch with what is fundamentally happening within us, not just a conceptual construction. This is non-dualistic uncensored information unfiltered by the lens of the mind. It is the actual truth of our present state of being

If I initially define myself as anxious, but then take the time to notice and become aware of what I am actually experiencing in my body, I may become aware of a hollow sensation in my chest, tightness in my jaw, and a feeling of tension behind my eyes. These are feelings that construct what I call the emotion anxiety.

The distinction is fundamental for transforming the information poor state we call emotion into the information rich resource of feelings. It is at the level of feelings where insight arises. It produces what the Buddhist teacher Thich Nhat Hahn calls "the liberation of understanding."

The key to accessing this information is to drop below the level of emotion and put your full attention on the specific physical feelings you are experiencing in your body. Stay with the strongest sensation, without pushing it away or skidding off of it. Inevitably insight arises; a thought, an image, words in the mind that relate to the source of the feeling. Perhaps insight into the historical origin of the generalized state will become conscious, information about why we are sensitive to this particular issue, or other material will arise which sheds light on our experience.

For example, diving below the catch-all emotion, "I am anxious," I drop into experiencing the specific physical sensation in my body of hollowness in the stomach. I stay with the physical sensation and as I do, in thirty seconds or so it changes into tears. Staying with the sadness, understanding arises. I am feeling the sadness I pushed down yesterday when my good friend Donny called and I didn't pay full attention to the painful problem he wanted to discuss. The embarrassing truth is I was watching a television program that interested me and I didn't want to lose its thread. I was distracted and didn't give him my full attention.

Of course, I should have said, "I'll call you back as soon as this is over," or turned the damn thing off and really listened. Instead, I gave insufficient attention to both. From one perspective it's okay, I'm not perfect, I make mistakes and I need not blame myself for this lapse in judgment and compassion. But Donny is a good friend and he deserves better from me. With this insight, I called him back and apologized. The incident actually served to bring us closer.

The work of feeling our feelings is an empowering and liberating activity. Instead of being the victim of emotional states, when we drop down into their constituent feelings, they become resources for growth and healing. If I had stayed at the general level of my anxiety, I would not have been conscious of what was truly blocking me.

You need not focus on all the physical sensations comprising an emotion to learn from it. Focusing on the one strongest feeling in the body is sufficient. If one sensation is not perceptibly stronger than the others, bring your full attention to any one of them. The feelings are holographic in that each contains all the necessary information you need, and all eventually lead to the same place.[1]

---

1. For a more detailed discussion Emotional Release Work, see Howard Schechter, *Rekindling the Spirit in Work* (Barrytown, NY: Station Hill Openings, 1995).

In our busy lives, we may feel we do not have time to engage in this work. What does that say about our priorities? In fact, growth work is not terribly time consuming. A few moments to stop the rolling wheel, to be quiet, and focus on what is really happening within us is sufficient.

The damage that comes from denying the emotions and not experiencing our feelings is too high a price to pay for the temporary bliss of ignorance. Until the source of the original feeling has been brought to light, it will stay within, agitating and seeking access to our awareness. The next time it may manifest in a more troubling form.

When a situation arises that consciously or unconsciously reminds us of previous difficult or traumatic experiences, particularly those originating in our youth, it reactivates old feelings. These feelings are arising to be healed. However, to avoid reexperiencing the pain, we often fall into a trance-like state. We unconsciously respond with the same programmed response pattern we used when we experienced the trauma previously. Because this type of reaction is not a choice based on the present situation, it is unlikely to meet the demands of the immediate challenge. The current circumstances are unique to this moment, while a reflexive trance-like reaction is a response to a different set of circumstances.

The original reaction to a trauma served to shut out the feelings because, at the time, they were overwhelming. If we have that same reaction in the present situation, we recreate the numb and frozen response pattern.

One way to free ourselves from this type of constriction is to feel the frozenness itself. What is the sensation in the body? Through this we may recall scenes from the earlier trauma, remember forgotten details, and become aware of how different we are in the present. Insights may arise and release can follow. The process of feeling the frozenness may generate more and different feelings. If we feel each new feeling that is generated, more insight and release will follow. Over time we continue until our reaction in the present is based wholly on the present and not a hypnotically programmed reaction originating in another time and place.

The reflexive response pattern can be a particularly debilitating factor in relationships. When our partner does something that unconsciously recalls a previous painful experience, a reflexive response pattern may emerge. The reflex is seldom helpful because the action toward our partner is not to him or her but to another person and a previous event. Thus we "objectify," or transform our partner from a person into a symbol. The diminishment of the other to the level of object may create a strong reaction in them as well, further contributing to a destructive downward cycle.

When my partner Barbara is frustrated out of her own personal dynamics, she sometimes gets short with me in her language. When this happens I have the tendency to react strongly, out of proportion to the actual words spoken. I fall into my reflexive reaction countering with strong words. I get hurt and, without making a conscious choice, withdraw behind an impenetrable wall. That wall protected me as a child, it was a shield from the verbal abuse I suffered then. But in the present it is dysfunctional because behind that wall I am distant and unavailable for reconciliation.

My pattern of withdrawal triggers the abandonment Barbara felt in her youth. It calls forth her frozen feelings and reflexive responses. We are then like two programmed robots, pressing each others buttons, and getting predictable but unpleasant responses. When the behavior remains unconscious, it insures a constantly escalating cycle of destructive conflict.

The way out for me, for Barbara, for all of us is to have the presence of mind and the courage to fully feel the initial numbing as it begins, before the reflex and cycle gains its hold on us. I can now feel the physical sensations in my body as I start to withdraw. But it is very hard and progress is slow. Previously, the reflexive action was so strong that there was no awareness of the slide into trance, just a seamless transition from hearing the harsh words to my closing down. Graduually, I am gaining time to notice the pattern and as a result I'm becoming less a slave to reaction. This incremental healing has helped me and the quality of our relationship.

This process feels like mining. I chip away at the ground of reactivity and each time I can see a little progress. Instead of unconsciousness, I open up space to maneuver. I have more choice in my responses. I am gaining self-knowledge and freedom. I am reminded of a line from a Bruce Springstein song, "What you don't surrender, the world will strip away."

Naturally, we open more easily to pleasant feelings than difficult ones. Have you noticed how fleeting these good feelings are, how rapidly they fade into oblivion? It is exactly because we are willing to, and do, open to pleasant feelings that they tend to diminish rather rapidly. If we were to open to the same degree to our unpleasant emotions, they too would diminish quickly instead of backing up like pressurized water in a closed pipe. If we open the valve and allow the flow of feelings, the pressure is released and the tension is diminished.

Despite our propensity to welcome pleasurable emotions, our cultural conditioning encourages us to keep even those emotions under control. Extreme emotions of any kind are seen as inappropriate. We even limit the extent to which we allow ourselves to enjoy the fullness of our delight. Most of us have learned to keep the door partially closed to ecstasy and shut almost completely to anger, sadness, and fear.

When you feel the deep satisfaction of seeing your child take her first tentative steps, the experience is beautiful. If in that moment we fully open to the feeling in our body, the experience can be even more profound. When I allow myself to do that, I frequently feel an expansion in my chest. If I stay with that feeling, inevitably the sensation of flight arises within me. The grace and freedom of this soaring sensation is one of the true joys of my life.

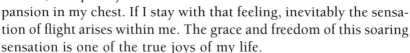

the eagle soaring

i went out with michelle
to see a friend
and have dinner

our first time "out"
just father and daughter
papa and little girl

she sat tall
and i was full

she sat tall
and joy
overwhelmed me

my chest became the sky
and my soul
the eagle
soaring in it

Stories

OUR HABIT, WHEN WE have problems in our lives, is to construct what I call stories. When we experience a difficulty, we automatically turn to the mental channel to "figure it out." We arrange the elements of the problem about which we are conscious into a logical order that fits together like a story. Then we analyze the story as the basis upon which to construct solutions.

The weakness in this approach is that we are seldom conscious of the all the key elements that constitute the problem. Nor are we fully aware of how they are connected. Our logical construction, therefore, becomes just a story that we take to be real. Unfortunately, it is closer to fiction. It is seldom an accurate representation of the full and true nature of the problem.

Further, as we all know from experience, using only the mental element we seldom arrive at a clear solution to the emotional problems disturbing us. Instead we get a muddle of alternative and conflicting solutions pointing in different directions. Each solution, as often as not, has as many points in it's favor as against it. We are left tired and confused.

We do better by supplementing the mental channel with the emotional one. When we drop below the level of story into feelings, we access information that has not been available to our conscious awareness. Because of the synthesizing nature of this intuitive insight, clear effective solutions may arise whole and complete.

Viewed correctly, personal problems, despite their unpleasant and confusing nature are allies in achieving balance. They arise to allow us to understand the deeper events unfolding within us. If we approach problems by addressing their feeling roots and refrain from total belief in our stories, we can make rapid progress in achieving the harmony we so richly deserve.

This was symbolically portrayed for me in a dream. I was in an open field. There was a huge concrete structure in the middle and I was stuck on a track circling it. I would repeatedly bump into the structure and hurt myself. I shook each collision off and began the circling pattern again. I continued to run around the structure until I bumped into it again, hurting myself once more. I was stuck in an endless loop of running around the structure, bumping into it, and hurting myself.

When I awoke and considered the dream, its meaning became clear. The open field represented infinite possibility. The structure was the "story," five "stories" high. The running around was the fruitless attempt to logically figure things out. My figuring did nothing to move me into the open field of possibility, nor alter the shape of the story, nor reduce the pain it caused me as I regularly bashed into it. My "solution" would have been to take the structure down at its foundation or stop running around it.

Sometimes the emotional release process does not provide solutions to our problems; it "disappears" them. What was previously defined as a problem is no longer seen as a one.

Barbara and I lead workshops at Esalen Institute in Big Sur, California. We teach group facilitators how to better guide their clients beneath their stories into the emotional roots of their conflict. This is a wonderful group to work with because they are already aware that problems are not solved at the at the level of the client's story. They know from personal and professional experience that one must dive below the surface, and they are willing to plunge themselves.

The five-day workshop gives every one the opportunity to address their most pressing dilemmas. The necessity for emotional release work becomes clear in this setting. All of us bring our anxiety and mental level constructions to the seminar with our luggage, hoping for a quick and painless solution. Each person begins their work by sharing their story. Quickly, it becomes apparent that progress will not be made at this level. Then, we are ready to dip into the pain where the healing and growth begins.

An illustration is the case of a workshop participant named John, a young man from Los Angeles. English by birth, he had moved to the U.S. after marrying his American sweetheart. John was troubled by the "problem" of whether to expand his construction business or keep it at its present level. This is a logical enough problem, apparently amenable to business level analysis. Yet the dilemma was causing him a great deal of confusion and a solution had evaded him for many months. He began by telling the group the details of his story; the state of the economy and construction market in Southern California, his financial obligations, the quirks and strengths of his employees, equipment headaches, and so on.

It is important to honor this first story-telling step, letting people talk through the whole story and listening attentively. We need for our stories to be heard. They are our creations, and having lived with them a long time we grow attached to the illusion. It feels bad when the listener disregards our stories to guide us deeper before it is the proper time. We don't feel respected and may well reject the guidance.

After John talked the narrative through, his energy settled and he became quiet. "Okay," I said, "let's go at this in a different way and see if we can shed some light on it." Slowly, I guided him into feeling his feelings. He was open, so the process moved quickly. He felt a strong sensation in his head. After he stayed with that for a bit, a phrase arose within him and he spoke it quietly. "I see," he said, " I see." The words were accompanied by the sound of a deep releasing breath.

"What do you see, John?" I asked. He said, "I don't have permission." I asked what he meant by that and he said, "I understand the problem about this business expansion thing." He proceeded to tell us that his father died when he was seven years old. "My mother was in constant fear that the family wouldn't have enough to survive, she played everything very close to the vest. I never got permission to risk."

John's dilemma and its solution were not about business at all, but about personal history. Its source and solution were accessible through his body. "I know I can do this. It will fall into place," he said. "I always knew I wanted to expand, but I was afraid to try so I made up reasons to confuse the issue. Now I know I can do it. I'm ready to move on this thing." He lapsed into a quiet reverie. He was integrating what he had just learned about himself. He said, quietly, "Yes."

"Louder," I urged.

"Yes," he said with more conviction and force.

"Louder John," I urged again.

And he screamed with full abandon, "Yeeeeeeeeessss."

There wasn't a dry eye or an unsmiling face in the room because we all knew that the problem and the story were gone. John would begin growing his business as soon as he got home. The details of that, how he would do it, was just a matter of putting one foot in front of the other.

the Source

We fuss on the surface
we fight
we make war
over issues

but really, there are no issues
there is only Knowing
and Forgetting
we are Divine Spirits
God in the body

destined to bloom
flower
fruit
and decay

so, when nations are at war
or people fight
let's not speak of
"it's because
blah blah blah"

or, "he said that she said
blah blah blah."

No!
It's not about reasons
it's Ignorance
or Forgetting

Resolution lies in mutual remembering
I am ESSENCE
You are GOD

We are all Divine beings
equal

Emotional release work leads to a gradual clearing of inner restrictions and an overall diminishment of emotional blocks to being in the present. As the martial arts masters teach us, we must be in the present to successfully face the challenges the present brings forth. From a spiritual perspective, the emotional release process allows us to gradually lift the veil interfering with seeing and identifying ourselves as Essence.

Spiritual Work Only

THERE ARE THOSE who believe that heart work, emotional release, is not required because spiritual practice is the only form of inner work necessary. Everything is fundamentally Spiritual, the argument goes, attending at any other level is illusion. All problems are inherently spiritual problems, and therefore all solutions must be spiritual solutions.

The view that Spirit is all and that other levels are merely illusion may in some way be true, but we must also honor the reality of this body and personality. It does not work to ignore the other levels of our human being. Not the mental, nor the physical nor the emotional. In most cases, it does not produce effective healing or lead to more balance in our lives. It often produces the opposite, trapping us in dead end experiences.

The belief that spiritual practice is the only kind of inner work necessary may be true for those who have already passed through the constrictions developed in this embodied life or who react to every situation with total equanimity. Since few of us fall into those categories, the approach does not work for the rest of us. As long as we experience strong emotional reactions, either clinging or pushing away, there is still need for emotional work. When we are no longer reactive and can experience everything in a state of perfect balance, then we know we are ready to focus on spirit alone. Until that time, our work must include going through the emotional barriers not around them

A dear teacher of mine, Harry Sloan, used to say, "You can't check directly into the OM Hotel." You must do the work of remaining with the emotions, dropping into the feelings, and then you will accumulate the currency for your stay.

Physical Pain

ONCE WE HAVE LEARNED to work with our difficult feelings as a doorway to insight, we can transfer these skills to better understand physical pain and what it can teach us. When we have a headache, a back spasm, a pounding in the knee, or a pang in the side we can treat that feeling just as we treated the sensations associated with emotions. Physical pain is another doorway to self understanding through the information and insight it generates.

The technique is the same. When we feel the pain, instead of avoiding it, as we are conditioned to do, we focus on it. We allow ourselves to fully experience the sensation rather than considering it as a discomfort to reject. We feel and drop into its particular quality and then notice what insight or information arises out of it.

For example, I had a pain in my back recently. When I focused on the feeling, into its specificity, I noticed a quality of debilitation and weakness. As I stayed with the feeling, I remembered that I had been offended by something a friend had said to me but at the time I suppressed it to avoid confrontation. I didn't honor my feelings, I just made it easier to get by in the moment.

That kind of behavior doesn't work for me anymore. When I am not truthful to myself and to others about the state of my feelings, inevitably my body will remind me through the voice of pain. There may be no apparent basis for the pain as in a headache or there may be an obvious intervening physical event like lifting something, bumping into the edge of my desk, or an unseen Frisbee clobbering me in the side. Mysteriously, whether the source is discernible or not, the process of focusing into physical pain often brings to consciousness information that helps me live more harmoniously in the moment.

This process works with illness as well. When you have a flu, notice what you are feeling in your body. Staying with those specific physical sensations, information about your overall state of well being, related or unrelated to the illness, may arise. This self-work also speeds the actual healing, because the emotional component plays such a big part in our physical health.

Though uncomfortable and unpleasant, pain and illness are more our allies than our adversaries. They carry information about which we are not yet aware and may not have been willing to accept. Because of the unconscious mind's process of signaling us first in quiet ways then becoming progressively louder, it behooves us to pay attention early, before the scream in the body gets obnoxious.

In the instance described above, before my back began to really hurt, there were other more subtle signals my body presented. In the moment of not speaking the truth to my friend, there was a sense of mild but clear discomfort. I disregarded and then denied that pain because I didn't want to deal with the unpleasantness stating my displeasure might have caused. Later, there was a general sense of malaise and then a headache. I disregarded both, took some aspirin and carried on. In order to shout the information more clearly to me, the discomfort turned into a very uncomfortable pain in my back. Fortunately, at that point I woke up and paid attention.

Much of what we call illness and pain is a cry for help from the emotional body. Physical pain is in part a directional device, informing us when we are off course. In its brilliance, it knows to turn up the volume until the signal is heard.

An amusing example of this is embedded in the continuation of my tale of the consultant and our conflict over fees. I have since been to court as the defendant. I consulted with a good attorney, prepared well, wrote out what I wanted to say, took an offensive stance and rehearsed my part thoroughly. I was ready.

The morning of the hearing I arrived at court and reviewed the calendar to find my case. It wasn't there. I studied it for five minutes and still couldn't find the case. I inquired with the court clerk and he was puzzled. He then looked up the case file and said, "Sir, the plaintiff has dismissed the case." The consultant had given up the fight. At first I was angry. As the song goes, "I took two bennies (amphetamines) and my semi truck wouldn't start." Quickly though, the joy of vindication arose and I wanted to throw my hands in the air and yell, "touchdown."

I drove home a man content. A few hours later, (this is embarrassing), my testicles started to hurt. It was a very unpleasant and unusual sensation. I haven't felt it since adolescence when we called it "lovers nuts." You got all excited necking with a girl but sex did not follow. What did follow was pain in the testicles.

To get some understanding of what was going on, I focused on the specific feeling in my body. Some interesting insights arose. The first thought, the most obvious one, was that I was all geared up and nothing happened. Then it occurred to me that I had been "kicked in the balls" by this man. He had taken a legitimate disagreement and turned it into a dirty fight.

Then, I saw that the feeling was so strong that it was simply screaming the obvious, "you've got balls." The process was giving me the feedback, "Yes you can stand for yourself in the tough going. You just did it. Now you don't have to prove it to yourself any longer." It is time to return to what comes more naturally, an easy going style, knowing that when necessary I can be tough in defense of myself and my family. The whole episode, particularly the instruction through my body, has been a great teacher.

CHAPTER SIX

Projections:
The Magic Mirror

"Why do you see the speck that is in your brother's eye, but do not
notice the log that is in your own eye."
The Gospel of Matthew (7:3)

P ROJECTION IS THE psychological term for a widespread personal and interpersonal process that can either create havoc or
enrich and transform our lives. Projection can destabilize us or be a
powerful ally for growth, depending on how we use it.

Projection is the process of casting onto others parts of ourselves
that we are afraid of or do not like. It is disowning what does not fit
our preferred self-image. When we deny a part of our self, for whatever reason, it will return to haunt us. Inevitably, it will be mirrored
back to us in our perception of another person. We can identify that
we are projecting by the highly charged nature of our reaction to
this mirroring process.

If we believe our projection to be what it appears on the surface, a characteristic in someone else which strongly repels or at-
tracts us, then we create an imbalance in that relationship and forfeit
an opportunity to discover a hidden truth about ourselves. When

we learn to recognize a projection for what it is, the process becomes a gift, a magic mirror exposing our unknown selves.

Certainly all feelings about others are not projections. We have responses to people based on preferences, likes, dislikes, values and standards. These are responses, however, not automatic reactions, and tend to be even tempered and composed. When responses become reactions, and have an intensely charged quality, it is likely they are fueled by projection. A friend described this as the 80%-20% rule. Twenty percent of the cause of the reaction originates in the characteristics of the other, eighty percent originates within us.

Light Projections

THERE ARE TWO KINDS of projections; light and shadow. Light projection is the process of casting onto others parts of our selves that we admire but which scare us. These are qualities we value but are afraid to embody. Living our greatness is a challenge we are sometimes not prepared to face.

Light projection is the central psychological process in hero worship. Whether it's a neighbor or an international celebrity, when we are intensely attracted to someone, it is probably because they are exhibiting a quality we admire in ourselves, but are afraid to own. If we make heroines of super models, it is likely we are denying the beauty in ourselves. If we see John Wayne as a hero, we are probably not fully owning our courage. If we idolize the caring sacrifice of Mother Teresa, it is likely that we fear that capacity within us.

Deference and esteem alone do not indicate a light projection. Such a response can flow naturally from shared preference. A highly charged reaction, approaching adoration, however, indicates the presence of light projection.

The strength of the feelings and charged nature of the reaction differentiates and identifies projections from other responses. "Reactivity" and "charge" are the two key elements signaling projection is present. When we are not responding but reacting, when the feelings are accompanied by highly compressed energy that we can sense in the body, we are probably projecting.

The charge in a projection is generated by the concentration of repressed energy escaping through the projection process. Like compressed water in a capped pipe, when it is released, the water forcefully rushes out. Non-projective responses, positive or negative, are more like water flowing from an open pipe, even and temperate.

WHEN WE NOTICE OURSELVES strongly reactive to someone else, it is a great opportunity for personal growth. It can be shifted from a moment of immense discomfort into an instance of transformation. It is the chance to gaze into the magic mirror and see a buried aspect of yourself. Projections are messengers from the not yet conscious directing us to recognize and understand qualities we have rejected and are now ready to reintegrate.

There was a time in my life when I was searching for more fulfilling and rewarding work. I wanted an occupation that utilized my gifts. Work that allowed me to be of service and was as challenging as it was rewarding. I was not aware at the time, but I was yearning, ready, but still afraid to unite who I am with what I do.

During that period, I attended a workshop presented by Harry Sloan. Harry was a man who had already united who he is with what he did and mirrored it back to me. My response to him was so powerfully charged, it was like falling in love. I put him on a pedestal and saw him as the most wonderful brilliant man I had ever known.

Harry's work was dazzling and his commitment total. With great speed he helped people release long-standing emotional blocks. What's more, his work had an explicitly spiritual foundation.

Harry died about a year and a half after that workshop. The opportunity to make him a living idol was erased, so the projection became more easily identifiable. I had the gift I saw in Harry, but it needed developing. I seized the opportunity to spend hundreds of hours analyzing and learning Harry's way of working through studying audio tapes of his sessions.

Harry Sloan lit a flame within me that has never diminished. Initially, I had not been willing to open up to the offering that he unmistakably mirrored to me. Gradually, the light projection awoke my dormant ability, and studying his work gave me the confidence to begin on my present path. My style has changed since that time, evolved and grown into a form that now is uniquely my own. But it took that initial light projection onto Harry to awaken me to a direction that has rewarded me beyond my fondest dreams.

alfredo's garage

we had an Argentine lunch
steak and salad
bread and wine
fruit coffee and talk

on a makeshift table
in alfredo's garage

a shop floor
full of filings
from parts
for cars

the scale is small
a few people
a few machines

but the natives are restless
it's better 'over there'

they want to run with the moderns
seeing but missing
their own beauty
in America's latest

they don't know
the price
in loss
of chatter
and the friendly relaxed

things that make it nice

they don't know
efficiency
can be a bore

and the end
of the Argentine lunch

When we haven't yet realized or are afraid of our own greatness, we may begin by seeing it in others. If we understand this process as a projection, it can serve as a point of departure for discovering our special gifts. If we merely idolize it, we may miss our unique beauty.

To get a sense of the light projection process for yourself, try the following exercise. Think of three people you greatly admire. Now focus on the specific qualities in these people that attract you. Write these attributes down. Now, look at the list, and with an open, playful, inquisitive attitude, consider the possibility that these are characteristics you have in yourself but have not yet opened to. What would your life be like if you did own these qualities?

Shadow Projections

Shadow projection is the process of disowning qualities in your self you do not like and that do not fit your preferred self-image. As with light projection, the action is mostly unconscious. After the initial rejection, we are seldom aware that we have relegated a part of our self to oblivion. The gift of shadow projection, if we recognize and work with it, is the opportunity to bring home the outcast child and make the internal family whole.

There are many aspects of our character which we do not like, which can be destructive, and which we don't want to grow or act upon. Manipulation, promiscuity, resentment and many more make up the illustrious field. Acting as if these qualities are not there because we don't like them, however, is a lie to our self that won't work.

Disowned parts may go away for a time, but they will not stay away. Eventually, they will rattle the bars of the cell of their repression and seep through, disrupting everyday life in unpredictable and often disturbing ways. Further, it takes so much energy to keep one aspect hidden from other parts of ourselves that there is less available for joy, spontaneity, and celebration.

Reintegrating aspects of character we don't like does not mean we must act them out in behavior. Because we recognize our lust does not mean we must be adulterous. Because we own our desire to be wealthy does not mean we must sacrifice our family life to achieve it. We retain the ability to choose, and that ability is more enhanced than inhibited by recognizing who we fully are, our darkest parts included.

Seeing the qualities within us as they are, not as we want them to be, allows us to construct our behavior more skillfully because we are acting with more accurate information. To act with the challenges visible, rather than hidden, is a great advantage. In the open they are less dangerous. Exposed, we have the opportunity to change them, heal them and transform them into working partners.

If we do not recognize projections for what they are, we may experience our lives as a series of unknown forces pushing us into seemingly unchosen behavior. We will remain judgmental of our neighbor's lust, but fail to see our own creeping toward a family shattering affair. We will righteously maintain an aversion to a business associate's greed, but be blind to the same desire twisting us toward some unethical and dangerous action.

The guiding principle here is: *when we experience an intense reactive charge toward another, assume it is a projection, and go inward.* When I am on my high horse about my neighbor's arrogance, it is a cue to look at myself. He is mirroring something back to me I need to learn.

I may be acting arrogantly or not. In any case, something in the territory of arrogance is arising for me to examine. Whatever I have hidden in this region is now coming forward to be seen, recognized, understood, and healed.

If my reaction to arrogance was not a shadow projection, merely a preference or standard, then my response, though negative, would be more composed and balanced. I would have noticed my dislike of my neighbor's arrogance and steered away from it, without the attendant reactivity.

It is hard to own projections. It is easier to believe the fault lies in the other. It is more comfortable to condemn the flaw in someone else's character than examine our own hidden darkness. As the quotation at the opening of the chapter notes, we prefer to "behold the remote events in our brother's eye, but consider not the beam within our own."

Working with Projection

BECAUSE OF ITS difficulty, working with projections is an extremely profitable enterprise. The mechanics of it are straight forward. The most difficult part is the first step, recognizing and being willing to acknowledging that we are projecting.

By looking first within ourselves when we experience the inner signals of charged reactions, we begin the process of changing our relationship with others by working with our projections. Rather than buying into the story we are telling ourselves about a friend, co-worker or partner, we check in with the feeling tone in ourselves. If we sense a strongly visceral reaction, we know we are projecting. Then we slow down, take a time out from our reactive response, and go deeper into our own feelings. We let go of the concepts driving the outward judgments and surrender to the quality of the feeling we are experiencing within. Slowly, insight will arise as to what is being mirrored back to us by the projection.

This process demands self-inquiry. As insight percolates up to conscious understanding, do not judge it. Just receive it. Judgment recapitulates the original disowning process and reburies the disowned quality. Embrace what arises, whatever it may be, treat it as a wounded child and love it unconditionally. Stay with it until you understand the fullness of its meaning.

Work with the accompanying feelings, using the emotional release method described earlier until you experience some sense of relief, bodily release, or reduction in charge. Paradoxically, by opening to the qualities we don't like, we liberate ourselves from their control. Through this process, we gradually free ourselves from the qualities we unsuccessfully suppressed, allowing them to fade away in the clear light of day. They are released through recognition rather than rejection. In this way, we cease creating magnets for their return.

Blame and criticism are two of the most common forms projection takes on. We often justify our blame and criticism with an attitude of self-righteous moral superiority. It is, of course, more agreeable to construct a story about the faults of another than own the intensity of our uncomfortable feelings. If you find yourself reacting with anger out of proportion to someone's actions, you can be certain you are projecting. It is the time to do your inner work.

Being a teacher in the field of human development, I have strong projections on other teachers in my field. The similarity makes them clear mirrors for my disowned material. They, more than most, reflect myself back to me.

Earlier I described the strong light projection I had on Harry Sloan. I also have a strong shadow projection on another prominent teacher in my field of study. I find myself extremely reactive to his writings, to people discussing his work, and especially to his celebrity. When people speak of him in laudatory tones, I immediately experience a charged reaction. The story I tell myself and others to support and rationalize my righteous indignation is that while his work is derivative and synthetic, he puts it forth as original and unique.

Where is this projection coming from? If I simply did not like what he was doing, I would turn from it. If my response was purely preference, I would be composed and unruffled in my discernment. But I'm not. He pisses me off to no end. The judgment is harsh and inappropriately angry.

Because I so want not to see what I am hiding, most of the time I'm in denial about this projection. I prefer wallowing in the lazy pleasure of criticism. And, there is the "twenty percent" truth in my observation to sustain and feed my judgments. The intensity of my reaction, however, is not generated by him but by my reflection in him.

When I gather the strength to own this projection, experiencing the feeling within me that accompanies it, I see the depth of my response arises from repressed judgments about my own work. It too is synthetic. A strong part of me doesn't like that. I want my work to be original and unique. I want to be inventive and creative, in the tradition of great thinkers.

So, when someone in my field is mirroring this synthetic style back to me, and masking it as original, I see myself, and I don't like it. The repressed energy rises to the surface and goes off like a rocket on the fourth of July.

Embarrassingly, this reaction is exacerbated by my desire to be recognized for the value of my work. I disown this ambitious part because I don't like it, it doesn't fit my self-image. But, like it or not, I have it, and denying it doesn't work. It raises its head whenever I see someone in my field who has achieved celebrity status.

So this teacher, of whom I am so critical, is a perfect screen for me. He reflects what I don't want to see, but need to integrate. I project in the cinema of my mind denied and hidden aspects of my self, seeing them depicted in living color, and providing the opportunity to reown them in a healthy way. Owning my projection in this way, energy is released from the low payoff activities of criticism and blame and are now available for the highly rewarding activity of becoming the person I want to be.

I have learned a lot from examining this projection. My work *is* synthetic in nature, and understanding that is important. I may prefer to be a pitcher but my skill is as a center fielder. If I want to play in the big leagues, I need to be a good center fielder. I can't do that without thoroughly understanding my strengths. I am a synthesizer and communicator. Recognizing that, I intend to synthesize in a unique and powerful way and communicate my message clearly and eloquently so it is easily understood and beneficial to my audience.

Also, knowing I have an ambitious nature, I shall remain alert and aware of this dynamic, and not allow it to unconsciously drive me into some unexamined activity that takes me where I do not want to go.

ANOTHER SIGNAL THAT projections are in play is self-talk. When you notice you are engaged in a conversation between yourself and someone else in your head, you are probably running off projective energy. When you are wrapped in a conversation within about what you would like to say to another, the unconscious mind is speaking to you, through the words you are saying in your mind to the other. We are making apparent to ourselves, information we need to understand about ourselves.

Projections unfold in a time release pattern like that found in the developmental process of plants and animals. Information is rolled out in a perfectly sequenced order. If we own our projections each time they arise, we will understand the appropriate next step for our growth. It will be a step that we are ready for at our present level. It is information that will serve as a foundation and preparation for absorbing and integrating information appropriate to the next level of development, unfolding from the teachings of earlier projections.

�֎ ✖ ✖ ✖ ✖

EXCERCISE

To experiment with shadow projections, think of a person in your life who is disturbing you. Someone who is "pushing your buttons." Notice specific aspects of their character that are disturbing you. With an attitude of open experimentation, notice what learning is in this mirroring.

Do you have those qualities?

Do they do not fit with your self-image?

Are you disowning something?

Do you have these qualities but are keeping them hidden from consciousness?

If there is a charge, and if you are honest with yourself, you will find some connection to your own character.

✖ ✖ ✖ ✖ ✖

When you are reacting, light is shining on a part of yourself that has been kept in the dark. If you have the courage to open to it, the knowledge flowing out of the darkness will serve you well.

Owning projections is an empowering process. Denying projections is a disempowering process. If we cast a part of ourselves onto someone else, the locus of control moves from us to them. We disempower ourselves when we needlessly relinquish our personal authority. So long as the source of our feelings is believed to be in the hands of someone else, we are powerless to make change. Worse, if you give someone the role of villain, you must assume the role of victim. If we do this chronically, our self-esteem will be seriously damaged, and efforts to make positive changes in any area of our lives will be compromised.

Owning projections is a de-victimizing process. If we grow our awareness and ability to identify the signals of projection, we can use the process to constantly expand our personal power. Self-understanding will increase and our relations with others will move toward harmony. We will cease giving away our power and become more fully the masters of our destiny.

We release the sense of being victimized by taking responsibility for our feelings. We are in charge of how we feel, so we are able to change it. No one else makes us feel bad or good, they just provide a context for our response. Ultimately, we do that to ourselves.

The Buddha taught, "Drive all responsibility into one's self." Let us look first and primarily within and take responsibility for our thoughts, feelings, and behavior. It's hard, it takes commitment and practice to change the habit of blaming others for our feelings, but when we get there it's worth the rigors of the journey.

The ability to take full responsibility for ourselves is what appeals to us in the otherwise destructive ethic of "machismo." The emphasis on domination and control is misplaced. But, the symbolic appeal lies in the empowerment this ethos portrays: take full responsibility for your life and be accountable for it.

The opposite phenomenon is our intrinsic distaste of whining. Whining focuses attention on another person as the source of our problem. Although it is sometimes a healthy release, chronic whining is often a way to disempower ourselves. It subtly programs us to believe that we are helpless and unduly influenced by another. We instinctively dislike whining because deep down we know that focusing on someone outside of our self as the causal agent, diminishes our ability to construct the lives we want.

I was working with a client, Jeannie, the other day on her feelings of anger about her recent jobs. We hit upon the sticky issue of "rank." Rank is a sociological concept defined as the place one holds in a hierarchy of power. It formalizes and institutionalizes power and powerlessness. In the army, for example, the lowest rank is private. The private holds a position of inferior authority to the corporal. The corporal has less authority than the sergeant. And so on, all the way up the chain of command. People with lower rank are more affected by people with higher rank than vice versa. Arnold Mindell, the founder of Process Oriented Psychology, emphasizes rank as having a profound impact on the psychology of the individual. As all of society is stratified by rank, it impacts us all.

Jeannie felt that as a woman the gender hierarchy put her at a disadvantage. Without higher education or formal training to move her up in the corporate rank, she felt relegated to the lowest rungs of the economic system. Being a woman stuck in low ranking jobs, working for men in high ranking jobs, she has been frustrated and dissatisfied. She feels more talented and capable than most of the men she has worked for, yet she is ranked on the bottom of the system. In this work context, her freedom and creativity are severely curtailed.

So, where does Jeannie go from here? The social or activist approach, if she chooses to take it, is to work on changing the system to remove this unfairness. Until that goal is achieved, Jeannie has alternatives to empower herself. Primarily, she can choose the way she responds to this inequity.

Jeannie can search within herself to discover how she is contributing to her own disempowerment and how she can counter it. When Jeannie did this inner work, went inside and owned her feelings and reactions, she saw that what she really wanted was to be out of the hierarchy of the corporate power structure completely. She wanted to work independently and be her own boss.

In the process, the insight arose that Jeannie's strongest negative reaction to the men she had worked for was their assertiveness. She discovered that her reaction was a projection about her own natural assertiveness that she had disowned since childhood. Assertiveness was a quality that did not fit with the feminine self-image she had constructed. Jeannie rejected that quality, but in so doing crippled herself in the world of work. To be a successful, independent entrepreneur and achieve her goals, Jeannie realized she would have to reclaim her power and assert it in her business.

Owning our projections and taking responsibility for our feelings requires a thorough honesty with one's self. Honesty, with your self and others, is hard to achieve. Yet, as we move towards self-honesty, it is liberating. Constrictions diminish and possibilities expand. We feel the excitement of new beginnings.

CHAPTER SEVEN

Relationship:
A Bridge to Balance

To confront a person with their own shadow is to show him the light.
Carl Jung

R ELATIONSHIPS PROVIDE A BRIDGE from internal harmony to external balance. Honesty with one's self is a necessary component of internal harmony and ultimately the key to satisfying relationships.

The root of honesty is honor. Those among us who are honorable are trusted. And trust is the fundamental component in building relationships. The honesty and courage to identify and own our projections is critical in two fundamental aspects of our lives: love and work. As Theodor Reik put it, "Work and Love. These are the basics. Without them there is neurosis."

Denial of our projections and the casting onto others of our disowned qualities is harmful in both these areas of our lives. In relationships, particularly marriage and family, projection plays a huge role in determining the quality of our connection.

We project most upon those who are in our presence most often. Because of the constant ongoing contact with family and loved ones, we project upon them more than anyone else. They become our clearest mirrors.

Projecting light qualities, we see sainthood where it does not exist. We sometimes do this with parents and older siblings. As we mature, the process inhibits rewarding adult-to-adult relationship with these members of our family. Freezing someone in a role of over blown esteem, we diminish ourselves, and inhibit our ability to establish a satisfying connection based on the reality of the present.

Projecting shadow qualities, we see in our loved ones the qualities we do not wish to see in ourselves. Our feelings and reactions can become strongly charged and negative. The judgment, blame, and criticism flowing out of these unrecognized projections can cause subtle to volcanic disturbances in relationships. The fighting, distancing, and animosity that erupt create conflict in our families and personal lives.

> ***morning magic fresh***
>
> in beginning is magic
>
> morning magic fresh
> everything is possible
>
> the day is strong
> we are strong
> morning magic
> dance of Hope
>
> everyday
> begins with Morning

We have all experienced this pain and examples abound. We project on our spouses and children many times every day. The strength of our reaction is in direct proportion to the desire not to see what is being mirrored back to us. If I am having a strong reaction to my wife's sadness, the source of that charge is likely to be found in my disowned feelings about sadness. I need to look there first before going outward with an unexamined reaction.

If I choose the self-reflective alternative, it is possible not only to grow myself, but also to dissipate the charge before it creates conflict. It is far more skillful to look within than to reflexively lash out, initiating a cycle of blame and defense.

Owning our projections is perhaps the most important thing

we can do to create positive supportive relationships. It transforms the projection dynamic from a liability to an asset. From a process contributing to the disintegration of relationship, to a platform for mutual growth.

The quality of our parenting is influenced by our projections. Because so much of our disowning process occurred in childhood, our children often become mirrors for our projections. If we have an intensely charged reaction to a behavior in our children, rather than a composed mature response, it is likely to be a projection connected to a part of ourselves disowned in childhood. For example, when we get really hot about undisciplined behavior in our kids, it may be that the freedom loving aspect of our self, which we repressed as kids, is arising to be reclaimed.

Unexamined reactivity will do little to help our children. It can, however, do a lot to alienate them and feed the very behavior we wish to see change. If we honestly confront the emotionally charged reaction within ourselves, examine it, learn from it, and communicate with our children about it, we can use the projection as a bridge to positively connect with them and offer direction that they may not feel compelled to reject.

When my daughter was thirteen, she was experimenting with marijuana. When I found out, I was angry, but most of all scared. I had been a marijuana user for years and though I wanted to stop, and had tried many times, I hadn't yet succeeded. I had a lot of stored up frustration and negativity about this failure. Fortunately, I realized that bombing Michelle with my projected anger wasn't going to help. With the motivation of a worried parent, I resolved to quit smoking. I did, and then we talked.

I shared my fears with Michelle about her smoking marijuana. I told her that her drug use scared me and it was important to me that she stop. She listened intently. There was no senseless laying down the law, no yelling or screaming. I shared from my heart and she listened.

Over time Michelle stopped using marijuana. Whether it was our talk or not, I don't know. I do know that at a minimum I allowed her experiment with marijuana to run its natural course. I did not intervene with my projected reaction in a way that would freeze her into an unproductive reactive response.

Noting that success, I tried to use a similar approach over the subsequent years when her behavior concerned me. I began by looking inside, then sharing my fears and communicating as clearly as possible what I would like to see happen. It has worked beautifully. Michelle is a wonderful young woman, with healthy values and a solid head on her shoulders. Now a college student, she has more freedom to make decisions for herself, with fewer parental controls to influence her choices and decisions.

Children instinctively want to please their parents. Innately, they do not want to hurt them. If we as parents own our feelings and share them with our children, we have a better chance of influencing them in a positive direction. Far more so than if we react out of unexamined projections, blasting them with our anger, and rigidly taking a position against which they feel compelled to rebel.

Projections also play an important role in determining the quality of our adult relationships with our parents and siblings. Growing up, our family relationships generated most of the repressed material that fuels our projections today. Because of this and the similarities of character and appearance we share, family members mirror buried parts of our selves and call forth strong projective reactions.

Anyone who has gone home for a family visit, had Thanksgiving with the clan, or cared for an aging parent is aware that something is going on in the interaction beyond the content of the here and now. We mirror parts of each other we don't want to see, creating a confusing atmosphere of interaction. For the brave of heart, it is also provides a wonderful opportunity to reintegrate and reinvent ourselves as whole human beings.

Every year my three brothers and I take a four-day holiday together. We affectionately call it the "Brother's Trip." It is a solidarity enhancing festival for us all. We talk and play and reconnect. As you can imagine, the projection process is at play among us. We are brothers. We spent our infancy, childhood, and youth together. Now, as adults, we are all mirrors for each other.

On every trip, over a long dinner or a stop in the park, the four of us take the opportunity to talk heart-to-heart, about anything and everything festering in the family. Things get cleared out and we go forward.

On our last trip we kept busy the entire four days and the clearing session never happened. I noticed my projections growing. I felt myself reactive and short-tempered and not the respectful loving brother I desire to be.

While driving, I practically bit my oldest brother's head off in reaction to him admonishing me for not giving good directions. He let it go, and things did not cycle downward, but I felt a nagging regret the rest of the trip.

Later, on reflection, I came to understand my reaction. Neal is 15 years my senior and by circumstance the two of us lived together with my parent's long after my other two brothers had left. Neal became not only my brother but a second father. Besides the love and joy it infused, I had a lot of suppressed anger about his authority over me. When it appears he is wielding that as an adult, my buried anger arises and I lash out.

I own that reaction now, and hope that the understanding and release will allow me to be a better brother to him.

On the "Brothers Trips" I always room with Robert, the sibling closet to me in age. With Robert, I notice I am reactive to his intellectual positions and arguments. My inner response is sometimes emotionally out of proportion to the actual content of the discussion. Occasionally, I have lashed out with an inappropriate, almost nasty, response. I have always loved Robert dearly, so this reaction confused and disturbed me. I didn't understand what was going on until I recognized the projection. Dropping into my feelings, I discovered a fierce competitive streak. I had not been conscious of any competition with Robert, but the projection brought it to light.

Robert and I were the most intellectually oriented of the brothers, as well as closest in age. As a child, I must have tried to out do him, to appear smarter and sharper, in order to shine more brightly to my parents and other brothers. My reaction to the little things we disagree on in the present turns big because I have suppressed that part within me. It didn't fit my self-image as an "easy going guy." But it comes raging out when I see it in Robert. Now, with more insight, I am hopeful I can turn this into play, as I reown and honor my competitive side.

The most interesting example I know of projection playing havoc with the lives of adult family members, is the case of two brothers who are partners in a multimillion dollar plumbing business in Utah.

Their unrecognized and unattended projections threaten to bring their relationship and plumbing empire to its knees.

All their lives Bob and Al were equals. Only eleven months apart in age they played on sports teams together, dated the same girls at different times, and worked side by side learning the plumbing trade from their uncle. The younger brother, Al, started a plumbing company while Bob went off to college. After two years Bob returned and wanted to join his brother in the business. Al agreed to take him in as a partner.

The dilemma was that over the years, Al secretly had never felt himself equal to his older brother. He saw himself as less skilled an athlete, less proficient a student, and less successful with the girls. Al resented Bob's dominance and success and he no longer wanted to live with that sense of inferiority. When Al let Bob in his plumbing business, he made sure he was the dominant partner. He structured the buy-in agreement that way. Al kept fifty one percent of the business, as well as the positions of Managing Partner and Chief Executive Officer.

Both Al and Bob thought the motivation for this arrangement was strictly business. It wasn't. Unconsciously, Al was structuring the contract so that he would finally be top dog.

Bob agreed to it, thinking the arrangement fair, considering Al had built up the business alone first. Neither examined the underlying dynamics driving the proposed arrangement. The structure placed Bob in a permanent underdog position from which he never ceased to rebel. The happy cooperation of their youth disappeared.

Since signing the agreement both brothers have been dissatisfied with their relationship and so have their families. The strain between the brothers spread to their wives, who had previously been good friends. The agreement was configured not to create an efficient structure but to compensate for an unrecognized projection. The friction it creates everyday in their lives is stressful, unhealthy, and sad. They love each other, but every day at the office drives them further apart. If they had seen the projection in the beginning, they could have avoided the split. If they would only see it now, they could heal it.

Projection in the Work Place

Projection dynamics play a significant role in shaping the quality of our work life. Because at work we are with people in an intense environment for so much time, projections run rampant. If we believe our emotional responses at work are really caused by others, then we disempower ourselves. We become helpless to change and unable to create a satisfying and rewarding work experience.

As a work place consultant, the most common problems I see are related to antagonistic relationships between co-workers, subordinates, and most of all bosses. Much of this dissatisfaction and conflict is rooted in authority projections.

Almost everyone has buried feelings about authority. As children we were powerless in relationship to the adult world. We had to deny our natural authority as a way to survive, especially in the family and at school. Often, if we asserted our personal authority, we were punished. Sometimes, when it was very important to us, denying that part of ourselves created scars. That wounding did not disappear, it just went hiding in the unconscious. As adults, when we become ready to reown our personal authority, it comes raging to the surface as a projection to be healed.

The formalized authority structure of the work place often mirrors to us this buried pain around personal power. When we encounter interpersonal dynamics at work that are not based on legitimate earned authority, but fixed simply in the formally defined system of power—as it was in the family and school—our buried resentment is awakened. And so we experience strongly charged reactions to those in authority out of proportion to their actual behavior. We find ourselves obsessed with rage against the boss. This level of emotional charge is rooted more within us than the boss.

While projection is the cause of much of our negative feelings about superiors, it also accounts for similar feelings about subordinates. When those who work for us do not act in ways we have instructed them to, or want them to, it calls forth unresolved feelings around power. Despite our superior position within the hierarchy, the negation of our authority awakens this discomfort in the present. Experiencing the buried pain is extremely unpleasant. If we are unaware that it is a projection, we may react with anger, blame and criticism out of proportion to the behavior evoking our feelings. We may become extremely disturbed, our subordinates may feel unjustly blamed, and smooth working relationships are disrupted.

With awareness, projections in the work place are an opportunity to see, release and heal dysfunctional patterns. Properly used, they afford the chance to live in the present and react to others as they really are, rather than the objects we have projected them into being. It creates the possibility of congenial and satisfying relationships in the work place, a more effective work environment, and a platform for personal growth that will spill over into all aspects of our lives.

It is rare, unfortunately, to make this transition from blame to healing in the work place. I consulted with a Washington state winery. The owner, a powerful authoritarian figure, had a close working relationship with a creative, somewhat submissive and rebellious wine maker. In the course of working with the business and these two men, I learned that the owner was much like the wine maker's father. And the wine maker was very much like the owner's son.

The wine maker, William, had a chronic inner ache because he never received from his father the affection and support he craved. William sought that in the owner, Phil. Phil, however, was unwilling to provide the loving support William craved, just as he was unable to provide it for his son. Phil had the capacity, you could see that in his playful moments, but he was afraid of his own easygoing side, he saw it as a weakness that could lead to disaster. When he noticed this softness reflected in William, it angered him and made it impossible for his natural good will to come forward. Phil kept himself distant and aloof, creating a perfect mirror for William to experience the disowned feelings he had stored up in response to his father's coldness.

Here was an opportunity for both men to heal some very deep wounds; a chance for both men to grow. By providing each other what they needed and yearned for, or simply taking the opportunity to understand the source of their individual and mutual pain, they could have been extraordinary allies.

It never happened. Both were too attached to fear and anger to look at the relationship from a different angle. They were familiar with what they were experiencing and more willing to live in that discomfort than explore their feelings, venturing into the unknown territory of owning their projections and reinventing themselves.

Eventually the wine maker was fired. Both men were embittered, angry, and cynical. The company lost a brilliant asset and they missed a golden opportunity. Sadly, this is not an uncommon outcome of projections in the work place.

BEYOND BOSS AND subordinate relationships, authority projections play a key role in diminishing the satisfaction and effectiveness of collegial and co-worker interactions as well. The group dynamics of management and work teams are often dominated by the projection process. People act out their power issues with each other as an alternative to, and at the expense of, the work at hand.

Anyone who has sat around a table during a business meeting knows full well that much, perhaps most, of the overt and covert energy is not about content, but subterranean power and domination. We can criticize these people as power hungry characters, or we can see them for who they truly are: wounded kids in grown up bodies trying desperately but ineffectively, even harmfully, to heal the wounding visited upon them years ago.

Projections around authority are not limited to the work place. They abound in all venues of our lives and play a major role in disrupting marriage and family. Because one of the most frequent unconscious reactions to repressed wounding around authority is to seek authority, it is common that a subtle or overt struggle for domination takes place between husbands and wives. If we do not own our unconscious desire to gain a position of dominance then we come to see conflict as the fault and failing of the other. Defining the conjugal struggle in this way, we attribute negative qualities to our partners and lash out in attack or withdraw in defense. We make them the villain, ourselves the righteous, all to the detriment of the relationship.

I have done this in relationship. I did not recognize my wounding around the abuse of power I experienced as a child in my family, or that I was projecting it onto my spouse. I made her the blackguard. I stopped seeing her for who she is, and created an illusion that mirrored my repressed anger and struggle for control. I saw her as the domineering woman and me the underdog male.

In fact, the image of fair-mindedness was my way of avoiding and denying my projected feelings. I was comfortable with my role. It made me feel righteous in a superficial way. Maintaining it, however, did not help me, her, or the relationship.

Being Projected Upon

In intimate relationships and work, disruptions are amplified when the person projected upon senses that what is happening to them is unfair and out of proportion. When we are in the role of the person receiving the projection, we are seldom sophisticated enough to recognize that it has more to do with *their* process than ours. We feel unjustly accused and may become confused, defensive, and angry. The disturbance gets magnified because the person projected upon may attack in return, intensifying the conflict. Or withdraw and severe the connection. Neither response builds the relationship.

Also, we project when we are the person receiving someone else's projection. The interaction becomes a soup of feelings consisting of my projections on you and your projections on me. It deteriorates into a Never Never Land in which both people are reacting to something or someone not even in the room. Yet, we behave as if the matter is deadly serious. Both parties get hurt, but nothing is solved because the root problem goes unaddressed.

The long run effect in business of disowned projections is the creation of cultures emphasizing sabotage and intrigue: "The hurt I feel now, you will feel later. What you put unfairly on me, I will get retribution for later."

In the family setting, similar dynamics may develop, creating resentments that tear at the fabric of intimate bonds between partners, parents, and children.

To stand for ourselves and treat ourselves kindly, it is important to recognize when we are projected upon. If we can identify the energy coming towards us as projection, it makes it easier not to fall for the illusion and avoid a downward spiraling interaction. We can see the criticism as having less to do with ourselves than the dynamics at play within the other. It becomes possible to choose our response and create situations that support us, rather than automatically attacking or withdrawing only to awaken in the Never Never Land of mutual projections.

When those we work with, family members, friends, or anyone else reacts to us in an intensely charged way, it is likely the projection is emanating from their disowned feelings. In the moment, however, it seldom works to point out what they are doing. It adds fuel to the fire. People caught in a projection are operating with the superficial confidence of delusion, supported by strong rationalizations and a sense of self-righteousness. They see themselves holding the moral high ground and their anger as justified. Any comment that deflates that illusion will further inflame the situation.

There are effective alternatives. We can employ the skills of the emotional martial artist; stepping outside the circle of blame and defense, moving out of the path of the attack, and letting it slide harmlessly by. Our best defense is the certainty that the attacker is more trapped in their web of self-deception than we are in their blame. Armed with this insight, we can drop defensiveness, take care of our feelings, and wait for the storm to pass. When the charge dissipates a useful discussion of the projection may be possible.

Anyone in a leadership role or a position of authority must learn to skillfully handle projections if they are to succeed and maintain a sense of internal balance. All leaders are projected upon because of the authority that accompanies their social role. It is inevitable and unavoidable. Business executives, supervisors, politicians, teachers, doctors, lawyers, therapists and anyone in a position of influence will experience the projected negativity of other peoples' disowned pain around authority. If you learn to identify the reaction as a projection, you can avoid falling for the superficial story that there is something wrong with you, and retain the balance necessary to help and guide those you lead.

Transference

Transference, like projection, is a psychological term for another common process that can either disrupt or enhance the quality of our lives. Transference involves transferring our feelings about one person or event onto another person or event. If we have had a frightening experience with a doctor, for example, we may transfer that fear to the next doctor attending us. If a police officer has treated us badly, we may take that anger out on another police officer though she may be fair minded and just. If a child was bitten by a dog, he may panic at the sight of docile, child-loving canines.

The dynamics of transference are very similar to projection. So similar that for the purposes of this discussion the distinction, while conceptually valid, may be functionally unnecessary. In both projection and transference we react to one person or event based on another person or event rather than the conditions at the moment. Both have light and shadow aspects and most importantly, both can be worked with and learned from in the same way. Transference, like projection, can be a platform for growth or a destructive force.

Light transference is shifting the positive feelings we have for one person onto another. If I love and trust my good friend Billy, and make a new business acquaintance, Michael, who looks and sounds like Billy, I may unconsciously transfer the trust that has been built up over years with Billy to this new person I hardly know. Lacking the awareness that I am transferring trust rather than bestowing it based upon an examination of the actual conditions in the present, I may enter into a business deal with Michael unwisely. In this case, my light transference, or my lack of awareness that it is in control, may cost me a lot of money.

In shadow transference, we displace negative feelings from the past to an individual in the present. If I distrusted my friend Billy, and I transfer that distrust to Michael without seeing the clear signs that he is trustworthy, I may cost myself money by avoiding a profitable business arrangement.

Another example is my experience with my high school and college basketball coaches. I hated my high school basketball coach because he was arbitrary and mean. When I moved on to college to basketball, I transferred this aversion to the new coach, Frank Miller. He didn't deserve it. By the end of the first season I realized he was a kind and equitable man. He had treated me fairly and well and I did not return the consideration. I was responding to someone else. Through blindness to my shadow transference, I missed the opportunity to connect with a man who would have been a good teacher for me.

There are a number of archetypal configurations for transference. One is the young man transferring feelings about his father to an older man with whom he is close. This happens often in the world of sports. It is common for a young man to transfer feelings about his father to his coach. Similarly, a graduate student may transfer those feelings to his mentor, or a young man starting out in the business to his boss.

Another classical configuration of transference is displacing feelings about a parent onto one's doctor or therapist. This form is so common, that skillfully working with transference is central to the effective practice of psychotherapy.

Perhaps the most challenging configuration of transference occurs in married couples. Men tend to transfer feelings about their mother to their wife and women transfer feelings about their father to their husband. This delusion, obviously, can be very problematic and damaging to the relationship.

The poet laureate of Great Britain, Ted Hughes, published a collection of poems in 1998 about his wife, poet Sylvia Plath, who had committed suicide many years ago. In it he express the insight that had arisen to him about Sylvia's pain. She was transferring onto him, her husband, the dissatisfaction she felt for her father. In a press interview Mr. Hughes said, "She could hardly tell us apart in the end."

Without awareness, we may be treating our wives more like mothers and our husbands more like fathers than the real people and mates they are. With awareness and practice, however, transference in intimate relationships can be transformed into powerful learning and an opportunity to heal long standing wounds created in the family of origin.

To work constructively with transference, we employ the same methodology we use with projection. The signal that transference is in play is the presence of a reactive charge in the body. A visceral reaction out of proportion to the actual circumstances present. We need to learn to recognize when our reactions are charged, rooted in repressed historical material or a composed response grounded in the reality of the present. Having identified that transference is present, we slow down, go inside, feel the feeling, then learn and grow from the insight. It is the constructive alternative to flailing about as if the transference were real.

There is another, more complex way, beyond recognition and release, to use transference for healing and growth. Under certain conditions, transference can be used positively to rewrite our personal script, replay the movie, and reenact the original destructive relationship with a more positive outcome. Psychotherapists use transference constructively in this way. They play out the "good" father or mother giving the client the healing benefit of that experience.

The positive use of transference is not restricted to psychotherapy. When a mentor becomes the good father for the young man whose dad was a bastard, transference becomes an instrument for healing old wounds.

The possibility for this therapeutic outcome was available to the wine maker and owner discussed earlier. Using the framework of transference, the wine maker was transferring his bad feelings about his father to his boss. The owner was transferring his disappointment with his son to the wine maker. The opportunity was available for both to throw out old scripts and rewrite new ones. For the wine maker there was the possibility to experience a loving supportive father and for the owner the joy of connection with a son.

Transference in the marriage relationship can be used in this way also. If the partners are aware and willing, they can provide each other the love and understanding they may have missed in their childhood and youth.

Working with projections and transference is about staying awake to our selves, taking responsibility for our own feelings, and continuous learning. Remember the Buddha's teaching: "Drive all responsibility into one's self." We need to be responsible for our selves and our feelings. Our obligation is always to go inward first before pushing outward into the maelstrom.

It has been said that ever since Adam blamed Eve for getting us kicked out of the Garden, we have been trying to avoid personal responsibility. It's time to change that program. Take responsibility for what you feel, and make a better, more harmonious world for yourself and everyone around you.

CHAPTER EIGHT

Intuition:
The Still Small Voice

"Knowledge has three degrees—opinion, science, and illumination.
The means of the first is sense; of the second, dialectic;
of the third, intuition."
Plotinus

INTUITION IS DIRECT INNER KNOWING. It is immediate knowledge unmitigated by the thinking mind. It is synthetic rather than analytic, integrative rather than linear. It synthesizes and integrates vast amounts of information and produces clear concise information. Intuition is crucial in developing and maintaining inner harmony and outer balance.

Relying solely on the rational mind to negotiate the challenges of everyday life, is like going into battle naked. Intuition goes beyond the limits of logic and directly accesses the genius of higher Self.

From a spiritual perspective, intuition is understood as the language of higher Self: the communication link between Essence and the conscious mind. Intuition is the voice of our divinity communicated to us through word, imagery, and symbols. Suzuki Roshi, the Japanese Buddhist the teacher most responsible for bringing Zen to America, equated intuition with the highest spiritual state. "Enlightenment," he said, "is a state of perpetual intuition."

When we listen to the voice of intuition, we temporarily dismantle the habitual barriers between personality and Essence. In so doing, we allow ourselves to receive direct truth and guidance from the higher Self, uncensored by cultural conditioning.

The Chinese holy book, the *Tao Te Ching*, begins with the assertion, "The Tao that can be spoken is not the eternal Tao." Lao Tzu, the author of this timeless work, is asserting that the God Principle, the Tao, is beyond the boundaries of language and thinking mind. It cannot be adequately described or understood within the parameters of analytical faculties. It can not be communicated, nor does it communicate, in the direct linear manner of the thinking process. What the *Tao Te Ching* and other holy books assert, is that the God principle, our Essence, is revealed through the nonlinear intuitive faculty.

From a psychological perspective, intuition can be conceived as the voice of the "not-yet-conscious," or unconscious mind. In the unconscious mind is recorded, like footsteps on wet sand, the total of all impressions and experiences of a lifetime. The majority of this information is lost to the conscious mind or was not accessible in the first place. The unconscious mind has the capacity to recall, synthesize, and integrate this data in ways that go beyond the limits of linear thought. Through the vehicle of intuition, the unconscious mind communicates to the conscious mind a synthesis of experience, observation, and study applicable to the present situation.

The unconscious mind, to which we have little access while the conscious mind is in control, provides clarity, direction, and guidance. It accesses the perfect knowing within. We are our own best teachers. Intuition provides us a way into the answers that are already there.

A credo written by the English novelist and poet D. H. Lawrence illustrates the central place of intuition in the human experience. He maintains that the higher Self and unconscious mind define who we truly are as human beings. He believed it is critically important that we learn to access this reservoir to be fully alive. In *Studies in American Literature*, first published in 1923, Lawrence wrote the following:

This is what I believe:

That I am I.
That my soul is a dark forest.
That my known self will never be more than a little clearing in the forest.
That gods, strange gods, come forth from the forest into the clearing of my known self, and the go back.
That I must have the courage to let them come and go.
That I will never let mankind put anything over me, but that I will try always to recognize and submit to the gods in me and the gods in other men and women.

Lawrence begins the declaration of his most central beliefs by asserting his primary identity as a spiritual Being. When he writes, "I am I," he is using the scriptural sense of the word. "I" as Essence or unity with the divine Principle. From this the rest flows.

When Lawrence says, "my soul is a dark forest," he is integrating the spiritual and psychological perspectives on intuition. He equates the soul, the seat of Essence, with the unconscious mind. Lawrence is stating that Spirit and the unconscious are unified. The unconscious is a storehouse of spiritual truth and Spirit acts through it.

"My known self will never be more than a little clearing in the forest." "My known self," the conscious mind, the part of me that I am aware of moment to moment, is only a small piece of who I truly am.

"Gods, strange gods, come forth from the forest into the clearing of my known self, and then go back." Lawrence is speaking about intuition here. He is noting the magical process of communication between the unconscious mind, with its spiritually infused insight, and the conscious mind, with its rational analytical ability. Intuition comes to us, deposits it's wisdom, and retreats home, to the dark forest of the soul, where it is again inaccessible and hidden.

"I must have the courage to let them come and go." Now, the poet notes the difficulty we have in opening to the messenger of the unconscious. It takes courage to honor intuition because to do so runs counter to cultural conditioning. The bias against all that appears nonrational.

It is also important to let the intuitive faculty "go," once its information has been communicated. Not to grasp after the trance quality of intuition and become addicted to its high. Abiding in the conscious, receiving intuition when it comes, and releasing it when it is complete, is the proper healthy relationship between the thinking mind and the unconscious.

At the end of his credo Lawrence states, "I will never let mankind put anything over on me, but I will try always to recognize and submit to the gods in me and the gods in other men and women." He is reaffirming the authenticity of the unconscious and the revolutionary zeal we must have to live by it. He echoes his contemporary on the other side of the world, the Indian philosopher Sri Aurobindo, who said, "Intuition is the memory of the truth." Spirit and the unconscious, are the abode of Truth, and any facade emanating from personality that does not reflect that Truth must be resisted.

Fear of the Intuitive

UNFORTUNATELY, THE DOMINANT cultural paradigm reveres the thinking mind while demeaning the intuitive faculty. Rational analysis is hailed as exceptional while intuition is widely demonized. The rational mind is associated with good and wears the white hat of consciousness. The unconscious is seen as the dark seed of superstition and evil. In the mainstream, "logical" and "rational" are associated with words such as "wise," "well founded," and "level headed." Unconscious and intuitive are associated with terms such as "illogical," "nonrational," and "uninformed." One dictionary defines "unconscious" simply in the negative. "The absence of thought."

There is no denying that we have made great material progress with our reason-based model of knowing. It is equally clear that we have paid a high price for it—disconnection from our sacred selves. It is time to reintegrate intuition into our social and personal capital. Time to remember that we can be successful in the material world and achieve inner harmony and outward balance at the same time. To do so, we need to honor intuition.

More powerful than cultural conditioning is the innate fear of the unknown. The unconscious is by definition unknown. Until we learn to befriend it through intuition, we will tend to avoid it. We see our unconscious, the hidden self, as an instinctual brute. The barbarous animal menacing at the gate of reason.

Our unconscious is not inherently menacing. More than anything it is the Divine repository of our essential goodness. In his book the *Third Millennium*, Ken Carey describes this, using the term spontaneity to stand for intuitive based action.

> You have been conditioned to fear what you might do if you were to act spontaneously, but such fear is based upon a lie. You are not evil at your core, not forged in sin. The universe has created in you not a demon or a fool but a magnificent luminous being. You share eternity's creative power and the wondrous beauty of time.

Most of us have learned in childhood to fear and reject our intuitive selves. The logical thinking mind alone, we are taught, is the only appropriate source of knowledge and action. This is a great shame and enormous loss. As children, we swim in the sea of unconscious knowing. We have direct access to our inner truth and we effortlessly blend the unconscious and conscious mind into one. Later in childhood, when logical thinking begins to become more well established, we have the opportunity to powerfully integrate the two. Instead, we learn to discard the intuitive and rely solely on the rational.

For most of us this shift is slow, incremental, and subtle. I remember clearly, however, the moment which sealed the process in me. My sixth grade science teacher, Miss Rubin, was the perpetrator. The date was October, 1957, and the Soviet Union had just launched Sputnik, their first space satellite. They had "beat us" and there was an air of fear and panic in the country. I can see Miss Rubin standing in front of the class haranguing our inadequacy. "Now the Reds will be on us and crush us. The Russians are in the sky and can drop the bomb whenever they want."

Miss Rubin paced the room. Her face grew redder. She was a little women but she pulled herself up big and shouted through her fear, "You kids. You're no good. You don't know enough to save us. You don't know science. You don't know math. If we leave it up to you we're dead."

Miss Rubin went on terrorizing us and in the space of a few days accomplished what is normally a slow incremental process. We were to leave our childish sea of inner knowledge, climb onto the shore of strict reason, and become expert at logic, science and technology. Supposedly, it was our only hope. She got that wrong.

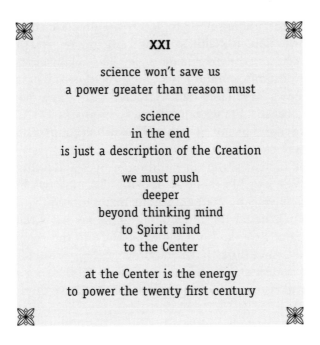

XXI

science won't save us
a power greater than reason must

science
in the end
is just a description of the Creation

we must push
deeper
beyond thinking mind
to Spirit mind
to the Center

at the Center is the energy
to power the twenty first century

The Partnership of Intuition and Reason

WHAT MISS RUBIN did not understand is that intuition and thinking mind are like perfect lovers. Two distinct entities that make consummate partners. They are neither competitors nor antagonists. One is no better than the other. They are different, having distinct qualities and serving different functions. Both are critical for inner harmony and outer balance.

The most effective approach to reintegrating intuition into our lives, is to strengthen its partnership with reason. Partnering the thinking and intuitive faculties allows us to use each in accordance with its strengths.

The thinking faculty excels at fine distinctions and incisive comparisons given a limited data set. The thinking mind's strength is also its weakness. It is limited by its linear and dualistic logic and in its ability to process large amounts of information at once. It is further limited by its censoring function. It will reject information, simply not process it, if it is not compatible with its overall world view.

Intuition has different strengths and limitations. Intuition reaches into the unconscious to access an almost unlimited quantity of information. It synthesizes and integrates it to produce insights not restrained by dualistic logic. The unconscious does not evaluate the separate components of information as better or worse, but combines all available data elements into a new whole. Intuition has no censoring mechanism and so produces its truths in full. Whether we like it or not, whether the truth is compatible with our moral and ethical criteria or not, we get it.

Overall, logic is better for building bridges and fixing roads. As we in the West excel in this way of using the mind, we build better bridges. We have generated enormous material wealth.

Intuition is better for understanding the nature of the universe, the meaning of love, and our personal place in the cosmos. Traditionally, Eastern cultures have emphasized the spiritual and the intuitive. As a result they have excelled in addressing the larger philosophical issues of life, and may be said to have produced great inner wealth.

What remains to be achieved is the union of thinking and intuition, the blending of East and West.

Sigmund Freud, the man most responsible for bringing the unconscious into mainstream discussion, viewed the partnership between the unconscious and the thinking faculty in the following way: ". . . *in the small matters trust the mind; in the large ones the heart. . .*" Freud believed that the thinking mind is an excellent tool for analyzing the smaller amounts of data that constitute the decisions of everyday life: comparing x to z and deciding which one to choose. The unconscious mind through the intuitive faculty has the capacity to integrate large amounts of information accumulated over long periods of time, and synthesize it all into clear unified guidance.

Intuition is better suited to defining "what" and "where." The thinking process to defining "how." For the big picture—visioning, understanding purpose, and defining goals, the "what and where" of our lives—intuition is the best guide. For constructing plans of action and deciding "how" to reach those goals and destinations, the thinking faculty is superior.

Generally, the intuitive faculty is a better source for big picture examination and the rational faculty for detailed analysis. The former is best suited for choosing the destination and the latter for building the vehicle and getting us there. The intuitive can be seen as an overall guidance system; the thinking process as a moment to moment navigational device.

The intuitive and thinking faculties can partner when the thinking mind evaluates direction from the intuitive heart.

One may consider as a guideline for action, what I call the "listen-act-evaluate " model. We follow our intuitive guidance and act on it. Then, with the analytical mind we evaluate the outcome. Now, with new information added we listen again for guidance. We follow that direction in our next step and evaluate the outcome again. And so on. Partnering intuition and reason is essential for creating a life in balance.

The vision and inspiration that moves people to commitment, effort, greatness, and loyalty comes to leaders not only as a result of their conscious planning and analytical thinking, but from accessing their intuition. Leaders, for better or worse, derive their charismatic power and ability to inspire from their intuition. Through direct access to their intuitive knowing, they project vitality. This sense of aliveness motivates people to seek their own greatness and inspires loyalty to the common cause.

Accessing intuition, leaders manifest authenticity, a feeling that they are connected to their elemental nature. The action that flows naturally from this place inspires others to follow. And, because intuition is so central to vision, it is crucial for successful leadership. The primary responsibility of a good leader is helping to develop and holding fast to the vision of the group, organization, tribe or country. This ancient wisdom has been codified for thousands of years and was set out plainly in the Book of Proverbs. "Where there is no vision, the people perish."

Doubt, Proof, and Developing Intuition

RATHER THAN ACCEPTING or rejecting the validity of intuitive guidance based on evidence presented here, the best trial is to experiment with intuition your self. Use your body/mind as the empirical testing ground. Tune into to your intuition and follow it. See if it is helpful. If it is, you have gained an ally.

Experimenting with intuition requires openness. Receptivity and awareness are the two most important qualities in accessing intuition. Both must be brought to the experiment. Be quiet and still, stand bare and exposed to the communication from your unconscious. Listen for the inner voice, note the images emerging in your mind's eye, and feel the sense of your body knowing.

Pay close attention to the words and symbols that come through the intuition. Spend time with them and let their meaning gradually emerge. Notice if your intuition provides insight and guidance. Notice if you make better decisions and are more skillful in your relationships. Notice if harmony becomes more your natural state rather than a rare gift. If so, you have found an ally. Keep developing your intuition and it will become easier to access and more useful in your day to day life.

Developing intuition requires quieting the mind. Stillness is the context, receptivity and awareness the skills. Accessing intuition is a magnetic rather than a dynamic process. We don't go out and get intuition, we call it forth and receive it. We can't make intuition happen, we allow it to happen. We quiet ourselves, open ourselves, and pay close attention to the blank screen within us upon which inner guidance is written.

Practice is necessary to grow the intuitive faculty. Trusting the process is critical. During the experimental period, one must suspend judgment until sufficient data is in. The criteria for success is not simply getting it right the first time. Without trust and commitment, the experiment may be aborted too soon. The criterion for success is our ability to open, little by little, to accessing intuitive guidance and, step by step, growing the courage to follow it. It may take time to sensitize our listening to hear the still small voice. We may receive good direction, but misunderstand it. Because we are not accustomed to the dance, we may occasionally stumble in the steps. In that case, try again.

Because the intuitive faculty is not linear but holographic, it doesn't follow the lock step process of logic. Intuitive guidance is often unexpected and surprising. It takes great leaps. It may guide you to take steps that don't quite "make sense" in their own right, but if enacted will serve as the perfect jumping off point for the next appropriate step. This may be confusing and even unpleasant at first, but stay with it until you have proved or disproved its worth in your life.

As with learning any new skill, developing your intuition is best done in small easy increments. You are thirsty and want a drink, but don't know what to order. Turn inside to intuition and let it be your guide. When you have received direction, follow it even if it seems strange and contradicts previous beliefs. See if the guidance and subsequent action is satisfying. Your intuitive guidance may say Coca Cola, but you don't drink Coke and everybody else says it's not good for you. Drink the Coke anyway and see what happens. Does it feel right and good in spite of the contradictions and the censoring thoughts of your self and others? Bit by bit, you will develop your access, receptivity and data about your intuition. When it comes time to go for the big picture for which intuition is uniquely well suited, you will be ready, capable, and skillful in its use.

In her book *Awakening Intuition*, Francis Vaughn writes that there are three keys to learning how to use our intuition: Relaxation, concentration and receptivity. Receptivity is the master key. Without receptivity, intuition is like an underground stream. It's always there, but inaccessible.

What Vaughn calls relaxation I call stillness. What she terms concentration I call awareness, or paying close attention to the inner process. Through concentration, the inner guidance that arises through intuition can be noticed. Our thinking mind often creates a din like a blaring radio. To notice the quiet guidance of intuition above it, concentration is necessary.

There are various ways we receive intuitive information. The most common is through the auditory channel. The still small voice.

We may also receive intuitive information through the visual channel. Images or symbols may appear to our mind's eye as messengers of the unconscious.

The proprioceptive or body-sense channel is another way we receive intuitive information. Through the body we get a feeling of physical knowing. We all have unique body signals, but everyone shares the sense of "knowing" when something "feels right." This is the experience of intuition communicating through the body.

A PROBLEM THAT ARISES when people begin to experiment with intuition is how to differentiate between intuitive wisdom and random ideas of the thinking mind. How do we know the information is arising from our intuition and not from some other source? How do we know it is useful and true?

There are a number of ways to differentiate the true voice of intuition from the ramblings of the thinking mind. Intuitive communication has qualities that identify and differentiate it. The voice of intuition is never critical or harsh. It is always gentle and supportive. Even if the intuitive guidance is pointing us in a direction totally different from where we have been going, the communication will not have the feel of rebuke. It will be encouraging and sympathetic.

The feeling dimension is the key to identifying intuition. Intuitive communication has the sense of communicating with a dear friend or loving parent. We know we have received intuitive guidance when we feel as we do in the presence of such company. As the great singer-philosopher Janis Joplin said, "You know you've got it, if it makes you feel good."

If the information we are receiving is critical, harsh, or judgmental it is not intuition. It is coming from some other source, perhaps a wounded place that needs the kind of healing addressed by emotional release work.

When we open ourselves to intuitive guidance our body will often signal us that intuition is in play. It is like the click of a machine indicating the disk or tape has been received and is properly in place. There are a variety of such body signals. The most common is a releasing breath. A big exhalation, like that which accompanies a sense of relief.

Other signs include:

The shoulders may drop as if letting off a load.

The neck may go loose and easy, flex on the shoulders.

The whole body may experience an overall sense of relaxation, ease, or release.

These are all signs that you have just received the assistance of the higher Self through the language of intuition.

You may be wondering what job to select after having been offered two different positions. Your thinking mind has gone back and forth for weeks but confusion still reigns. For every strength you see in job A, the mind brings forward an opposite liability. The same occurs when you ponder job B. You have sought counsel from friends and family and for every opinion you get, someone else has the opposite advice. Your mind is in a whirl.

Then, you remember to apply for assistance from intuition. You stop, become quiet, still the mind, and consult your inner knowing. Without rushing, you open yourself to your own gentle guidance. Slowly, you sense it, or hear it, or see it. There is a sympathetic, positive, encouraging feel. "Don't take either," the still small voice directs, "they will both kill you with stress. Wait. The right one has not yet come along." You are surprised, you never looked at this option, it's scary, but there is a big exhaling breath. You feel a sense of ease and relief in your whole body, and you know it's right for you. Do you have the courage to follow it?

Types of Intuition

I SEE THREE TYPES of intuition. I define and differentiate each based on the time necessary to access each type. They are "spontaneous," "brief" and "focused" intuition.

Spontaneous Intuition

Spontaneous intuition is direct immediate knowing. It comes instantaneously, in a flash of sudden insight, without any attempt or effort to call it forth

All of us have had the experience of spontaneous intuition. Often the issues involved are minor. Occasionally, the insight is life changing. In a flash of spontaneous intuition people have become aware of their life calling. Inspiration for great artistic and scientific work may come through spontaneous intuition. Einstein is said to have originally understood what later became the theory of relativity in a flash of spontaneous intuitive insight. The design for the Golden Gate Bridge, which defied Californians for decades, is said to have emerged full blown in its architect's mind in a similar way.

The solution to problems that have plagued us for years may arise over a cup of tea or while doing a crossword puzzle.

I know of a case where a financially struggling business owner was in conflict with his workers for many years. Eventually the workers unionized, went on strike, and intensified the conflict. It became ugly and violent. At one point in the strike battle, the owner was so infuriated by the union's behavior that he went out to the yard where the pickets were gathered carrying a baseball bat. He drew a line in the dirt, and challenged any one to cross it.

In that moment, as he looked out at a sea of angry faces, everything slowed down for him. Suddenly and unexpectedly he had a flash of spontaneous intuition. He knew in that instant, beyond a certainty, that everything about the way he had been dealing with his workers must change. It was not self-criticism or regret, just a clear conviction that things must shift.

He dropped his club, turned, and walked away from that potentially bloody confrontation. He began changing the operation of the business immediately. Within a week he had settled the strike with the workers. He then sought experienced help to work on improving communication within and between all elements of the enterprise. Issue by issue, management began to address all the legitimate concerns of workers. Now, seven years after that dramatic moment of spontaneous intuition in that parking lot, he is a well loved leader, running a highly profitable business. There is an air of cooperation in his organization that brings a warm glow of satisfaction to the hearts of all who knew the business before that insight struck.

Because spontaneous intuition arises quickly and requires no conscious preparation to call it forth, it can catch us by surprise and be elusive. The insight arises before our normal censoring mechanism takes hold. It may be startling and therefore easily rejected or confused with a random thought. However, if the insight has an initial sense of correctness and ease, of supporting us, of being uplifting, then we need to bring our discrimination forward, identify that insight as valuable information from the higher Self and act on it.

There is a saying, "first thought best thought," that captures the usefulness of spontaneous intuition. Our very first thought is often generated by the spontaneous intuitive process. It arises to the thinking mind as direct, synthetic uncensored material. Once we begin mulling all the other possible options which the mind brings forward, the intuitively generated material fades into the background and gets lost among the louder voices of the thinking mind. I remember learning this guideline in school when I discussed with one of my teachers my difficulty in test taking. "Go with your first thought Howard, it's usually right." I followed that advice and my test scores and school grades improved significantly.

The "first thought, best thought" guideline is useful outside the classroom as well. If one wishes insight into an area where the thinking mind is confused, shift gears. Bring the subject forward for consideration but let go of the analyzing. Allow rapid uncensored associations to emerge. The spontaneous intuitive process will provide a wealth of previously unavailable alternatives to you for consideration. Some may be surprising because they are unfiltered by the inner critic, or because they are based on variables your thinking mind has not yet considered relevant.

The methodology is similar to the free word association process popularized by Freud and Jung early in the century. In order to cut through a patients habitual confusion generated by recurrent thought patterns, the therapist speaks a word and asks the client to reply with the first response that naturally arises, without censure. The client is urged to freely speak the response without regard for making sense, being proper, or worrying about the impression it may make. Using the device of free association to trigger spontaneous intuition, the therapist is able to help clients break through confusion. Revealing and healing truths emerge that the client otherwise would not have allowed in.

I discovered the usefulness of applied spontaneous intuition in an interesting way. I was part of a business training program. My group of trainers was trying to encourage business managers to become more aware of their feelings in the work place. We used a training technique called brainstorming. In brainstorming one asks the group to spontaneously call out ideas and the trainer writes them on the board. The technique was originally designed to stimulate creativity and get new ideas into play that would not be put forward if the analytic process were engaged. In this case, we asked participants to call out words that described feelings. The purpose was to get the participants attention on the subject, and warm them up for the next phases of the training.

I wrote the feeling words on a large easel pad as participants called them out and then hung the paper on the wall for everyone to see. According to the curriculum guide, that was meant to be the end of that particular training module. We were to proceed to the rest of the program.

After doing the exercise a number of times, it dawned on me that this brainstorming exercise was not a warm up or a preparatory event at all, it was the most profound aspect of the entire training. It was an informal word association test. It was as if we were in the therapist's office and I said the word "feeling," and then each person gave their spontaneous intuitive response.

It worked well because it was so informal and none of us realized how deeply we were hiding feelings. The words they called out, I came to see over time, were the feelings most profoundly affecting them in the moment, uncensored by worry, propriety or impression management. They didn't know it, but they were revealing more about themselves than they would ever have through the thinking process.

I moved the exercise to the beginning of the training and used it as a diagnostic tool. Through it, I came to understand what it otherwise would have taken a long time to discern; the emotional state of the group and the condition of the individuals in it. With that, I was able to shape the training to fit their true needs and be more helpful to everyone. The quality of the training improved substantially and the increased effectiveness of the program was substantiated by higher marks on participant evaluations.

Brief Intuition

"Brief intuition" is the second way in which the unconscious and higher Self speak to us directly, but not in the effortless instantaneous flash of spontaneous intuition. Brief intuition involves more focus. It requires consciously calling forth the intuitive faculty. The most common way to use brief intuition is in the question and answer format. We go inside, become quiet, and relax the thinking mind. We pose a question about which we seek clarity and wait receptively for insight to arise. Generally, the information from the higher Self will emerge quickly.

For example, we may be contemplating relocating. We are confused and stuck in the rational mind's analysis of "yes" and "no" dimensions of the question. We go within, quiet the mind, and ask, "Should I move to Southern California?" Then, in a state of nonattached receptivity, with our awareness keenly tuned, we wait. We don't try to do anything or figure anything out.

Clarity will arise, but it must not be forced. With practice, one can easily drop into the necessary state of receptivity and readily identify the information arising out of brief intuition when it appears. It may not be a yes or a no answer. It may not even seem like a direct response to the question. But the guidance coming from your deepest synthetic wisdom will be exactly what you need to know in this moment to take your next step toward understanding and solving the challenge posed.

Brief intuition is particularly effective during times of day when you are already naturally in a receptive state. In the morning upon waking, or in the middle of the night when you are temporarily awake. Because you are emerging from a sleep state, the conscious mind is turned off. At such times, we have easy access to the not yet conscious. If you ask a question of yourself then, or a series of questions, you will be amazed how profoundly helpful and clarifying these answers can be.

Focused Intuition

The third type, "focused intuition," involves more complex, time consuming, directed methods for accessing inner wisdom. One example of focused intuition is the emotional release work discussed in chapter four. That method for drawing out the teachings lodged within our feelings by going inside and accessing their latent wisdom is a form of focused intuition.

What some people call "trance work" or "induction" is an excellent way to use focused intuition for accessing inner guidance. This method involves being lead into a state of quiet by a guide or audiotaped voice. Through suggestion we enter a state of deep relaxation. In that state, the mind becomes calm and quiet, opening access to the unconscious knowing and wisdom of our higher Self. The guide may ask focused questions to draw out information on areas we wish to explore. Or we may just wait receptively for the wisdom of the unconscious to bring forward what we need to know. The active and passive methodologies may be combined by starting with directed questions and then releasing them and waiting for guidance to emerge.

When presenting the "Rekindling the Spirit in Work," workshop, I guide everyone into a relaxed receptive state. Then, I ask them to see their perfect work setting, walk around it, and explore it in every way. Invariably the unconscious mind converts vague ideas of the persons' hopes and dreams into concrete understandable images. Through the process of focused intuition, people discover their ideal work setting, work relationships, type of work, and structure for workdays. The inner guidance produces a sense of direction and strength for the next steps in their work lives.

Material emerging from a focused intuition experience is often information participants were vaguely aware of but had been blocking due to fear. They are afraid of the disruptive consequences the action resulting from this knowledge might have. If, for example, they had a vague sense that they wanted to do something out of the ordinary, like be a writer, the fear that such a desire will necessitate giving up their job and present life-style, causes them not to fully let out the dream. As a result, it lingers underneath, creating a hard to define discomfort, a sense of dissatisfaction that interferes with enjoying their life.

Using the focused intuition exercise, the censor is relaxed and the dream emerges loud and clear. Once it does, people are surprised to find that it is not dangerous or scary. In fact, it is enlivening and they are still in charge of their lives. They maintain their freedom of choice. But they have released the deadness that resulted from blocking an important aspect of their inner life, and gained the vitality of their dream. Invariably, people find that the dream can be integrated in new and creative ways that have not been considered before because their energy was tied up in rejecting it. The new, integrated dream maintains what they love and adds elements of their unnourished longing to enrich their lives.

Through the experience of focused intuition, people learn an important principle of balance: knowing and acting are separate mechanisms. Knowing that something is true does not demand any specific action. We can fully open to our inner truth and at the same time retain the freedom to choose behaviors that best support other truths for our selves and those around us. Understanding this principle enables us to fully allow in the brilliance of unconscious guidance, avoid the deadness of blocking our inner truth, and maintain the confidence that through integrating intuitive knowledge into our lives we will be continuously enriched.

Because we want to paint does not mean our choice must be to live in a garret as a starving artist. It means only that we know we want to paint. From there, the choice of action is separate and independent. We can integrate our desire to paint with other hopes and devotions, like providing for our families and the fun of a fast car. Intuition in its holistic wisdom will bring forward the previously censored truth and provide us with creative and exciting ways to integrate it into our present lives.

Focused intuition is a friend in our journey toward harmony and balance. When there are confusions about relationships, health, family, work, or any subject of importance to us, it is useful to take the time to go within. Our own inner wisdom has the answer. The unconscious repository of the higher Self knows the way out of confusion. It provides clear and trustworthy guidance that perfectly fits who we are. Advice from others is generally not worth much. Advice from ourselves is priceless.

I had a client who was the fifth generation owner and president of a multimillion dollar international family business. He was dissatisfied with his work and ready to leave his position in order to seek more satisfying work. He came to me for counsel. I didn't know what he should do, but I knew that within him were the answers.

My work was to guide him into his wisdom for clarity and direction. During a guided exercise, I led John into a trancelike state. Through suggestion I helped him relax mind and body. I asked a few general questions about the dilemma he had posed to prime the pump and then I kept quiet for ten minutes. In that time he roamed his unconscious and received its guidance.

John reported that during the experience he went back in time and saw himself playing with his grandfather, a peaceful and wise man who had been one of the first Western students of Buddhism in early twentieth century Europe. John saw himself with his childhood clarinet, playing blissfully and experiencing the happiness and fulfillment he only felt when playing music, an activity he had not engaged in for many years. As John recounted the inner journey, I could see the joy reflected in his countenance. He was at peace, at ease and happy. He glowed with an inner delight and pleasure.

I asked John to go back inside and ask the image of his grandfather his belief about John staying in the business. Should John get out of the business? The immediate answer from within was a resounding No. "No, don't leave it, fix it," said the voice of intuitive wisdom, spoken through the words of this wise inner teacher figure.

Directing John to stay in the trance state, I asked him to imagine what it would be like to remain in the business, running it, fixing it, changing it from what it was to a place where it is possible to experience the kind of joy he was experiencing now. I again left him alone for some time to quietly dwell in his unconscious wisdom.

By the time John returned to a waking state there was no more doubt, confusion, or worry. He was thoroughly committed to staying with the business and transforming it. Just before he left, John said to me, "I'm going to change it by changing myself." I got goose bumps.

Unfortunately, even intuition is not the legendary silver bullet. Intuition does not always provide the solution or the right answer immediately. Over time, if called upon regularly and with integrity, it will move you closer to the right answers.

About twelve years ago, some time after I was divorced, I was confused and in a lot of pain. There were a number of different women in my life and I seemed to be trying to solve my sorrow by adding more as fast as I could. I was creating more conflict, of course, each time I did that, and it only got worse.

Every time I went inside about this, a still quiet voice said, "Barbara, Barbara." Literally, like that, a voice saying, "Barbara, Barbara." I was surprised every time. Of the women I was involved with, Barbara was the least like women I had previously been attracted to. She was not the woman I would pick with my thinking mind, using its habitual criteria. But, thinking wasn't working very well for me anymore, so I followed its guidance. Often, it takes an emotional breakdown before we wake up to the faultless ally we have inside and surrender to it.

I disentangled myself from the other relationships and committed myself to the one with Barbara. It has been one of the best things I have ever done in my life. A decision far beyond the capacity of my thinking mind. It was directed by higher intelligence and communicated to me by the still small voice of intuition.

We are a wonderful match. We share the joy and the pain. If I had left that decision to the thinking mind we would not have made this partnership. It took a greater wisdom and intuition to bless me with it.

Exercise

If you want to try a simple focused intuition exercise, bring forward a problem in your life about which you have considered a number of different solutions. Take some time getting quiet and thoroughly relaxed. Review the problem briefly, imagining that each of the solutions is a trail going into the woods in front of you. In your minds eye, in a state of relaxed receptivity, walk down the first path, representing the first solution. Notice what you see and hear and take in all the information that comes to you in whatever form. What did you learn about that first option? Then, maintaining that state of quiet receptivity, do the same thing for the second trail and the third until you have completed all of the known options. Finally, walk down a new trail, one you have not seen before, representing a solution you have not yet entertained, and open to the intuitive wisdom that arises there.

When you are finished, remain quiet, focus inward, and consider the information you have received. Without effort let your unconscious integrate what you learned and provide you with guidance. This exercise produces helpful results and will give you an excellent introduction to the use of focused intuition.

Practicing and Stimulating Intuition

IT IS POSSIBLE to both practice and stimulate intuition so that it comes with greater ease and is readily available when we wish to access it. Practice, as with any other skill, involves using our intuitive faculty as frequently as possible, and in as many different ways and situations as possible. Opening to it, trusting it, and testing it against our experience is the formula for personal experimentation with intuition.

You can stimulate the frequency of spontaneous intuition in a number of ways. Creative activities such as drawing, painting, sculpting, dancing, and writing help put the logical faculty at rest and move the not yet conscious into the foreground. Dwelling in the trancelike state of creating, spontaneous guidance arises to direct our art and give us direction for our daily life.

Movement and touch also stimulate intuition. Both diminish the hold of the analytic mind and allow not-yet-conscious material to come forward. Movement in the form of sport, exercise, yoga, or dance puts one directly in touch with the unconscious. Almost all athletes, even us weekend joggers, know that unexpected and helpful insights arise to what previously seemed like insoluble problems, during a morning run, or right after a swim or a bike ride.

It works similarly with touch. When we are experiencing a massage, or a simple shoulder rub, the grip of the thinking mind relaxes and we can drop into a light trance if we open to it and allow it. In that state we have access to our intuition, much like that experienced in focused intuition. I have often gotten clear about some difficult situation in my life while in the light trance generated by the relaxation of massage. It has happened getting a haircut when I give myself over to the pleasantness of that touch. Even, believe it or not, sitting in the dental chair when the procedure is painless and the atmosphere is relaxing. You never know where intuition may strike.

Any time we "change channels" and experience the environment through a different sense channel than normal, the analytical and censoring processes go on hold. Then, the doors to our inner wisdom open wider. If you generally experience the world through your sight channel, switch to focusing on listening. Or smelling, or tasting, or touch. You will notice that this channel changing will put you more directly in touch with your intuition. If you feel discordant about something that you have kept to yourself, try talking about it. If you have talked about it and no guidance emerges, try writing about it. Draw it. Color it. The shifting will soon produce intuitive guidance.

If you are confused about a life issue, try "moving it." Take a pose that physically imitates the way the problem makes you feel. Notice what flashes before your mind's eye. If nothing emerges, try moving it more. Allow the next natural movement to unfold out of the previous one, without design or forethought. Make a dance out of it. Wrestle with it if you must. At some point, with one of these shifts, insight will emerge, direction will arise, and harmony will be reestablished.

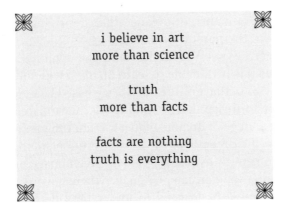

i believe in art
more than science

truth
more than facts

facts are nothing
truth is everything

Dreams and Dreaming

DREAMING IS A SISTER to intuition. It is a mechanism of access to the higher Self through the brilliance of the not-yet-conscious. Dreams have been a source of guidance and inspiration to humankind since the beginning of time. We would do well to pay more attention to our dreams, take them more seriously, and benefit from the magnificent guidance that comes to us on the pillow.

The essential function of dreaming is to restore balance. To some extent, dreams do that for us even when they are unexamined, by running off energy that needs releasing. When we examine our dreams and integrate them into our normal thinking process, they are even more valuable.

The dreaming process, through its language of symbols and imagery, provides information that we have not yet consciously understood. Dreams offer clarity, if we choose to receive it, about matters that are disturbing our harmony in the waking state. Dreams direct us towards paths that are supportive of our health, welfare and growth. They provide guidance in areas where direction is unclear. And, as in the projection process, they help us regain wholeness by pointing out the parts of ourselves we have disowned in our waking state as a result of self-judgment.

These functions are served through the communication of dream symbols and imagery. It is a language we are not accustomed to and may find difficult to interpret. As a result, we do not pay sufficient attention to the guidance of dreams, thus depriving ourselves of a powerful ally in the pursuit of balance.

It will serve us well to understand the symbolic language of dreams. Just as it is invaluable to learn Spanish when living in Spain in order to thrive in that culture, the image based language of dreams requires study to thrive in our waking life. Fortunately, it is easier to learn the language of dreams than a foreign tongue. All it requires is attention to the dream and the desire to understand it.

There is no absolute meaning to any given image or symbol in a dream. It is not a standardized language where a word has a specific definition that must be learned to understand it. The language of symbolism is particular to each of us. A car on a hill may mean one thing in my dream and another in yours. It depends on our individual unique associations with the symbols of car and hill.

There is no vocabulary, syntax or grammar to learn in dream interpretation. One easy way to understand the personal imagery of our own dreams is to use the brief intuitive process of association. Recall a dream you have had recently. Write it down. Extract the symbolic elements. For instance, a car, a hill, my friend Bill, a Chinese man and the feeling of loss. Now, freely associate with each word. Write down next to the word car your first immediate association. Do the same with hill, and so on until you've completed your list. That first immediate association draws forth the meaning of that symbol in your personal cosmology.

Now, similarly, quickly and freely, without a struggle to generate meaning, note what arises in your awareness when you string those symbols together into a story. What parable emerges? How does it relate and support your waking life?

Now, bring in the strengths of the thinking mind and examine the parable further. Study it closely and deeply. Analyze it to generate a higher level of meaning and guidance.

There are many other ways to understand dreams. They generally lead to the same goal. A useful and uncomplicated way to interpret dreams is through the Gestalt technique of dream analysis. Using this method, we take each major symbol in the dream and imagine it to be an embodied entity carrying information to us from the unconscious. We talk to it and let it speak to us.

Let the symbol itself, through your imagination, speak its wisdom to you in an uncensored, uninhibited way. We ask the car what it represents and what it wants us to know. We ask the same of the hill, the friend, the Chinese man, and the feeling of loss. We dialogue with each part and listen receptively to its wisdom. The symbol, as an embodied entity, is representing an aspect of our not yet conscious and communicates to us exactly what we need to know. That is the magic of dreaming.

CHAPTER NINE

The Healing Relationship

Who you are . . . thunders so loud that I cannot hear your words.
Ralph Waldo Emerson

U NTIL NOW WE HAVE FOCUSED on internal sources of harmony. Turning to relationships, we consider what creates balance in the external world—through connection with others.

The quality of our relationships in large part determines the level of satisfaction we experience in our lives. The joy of intimate relationships, the character of our friendships, the quality of our associations in the workplace, even the nature of our casual connections have a tremendous impact on our sense of well being. The quality of all these connections is determined primarily by our individual style of interaction, by the way we have learned to build and maintain relationships.

For the most part, little attention is paid to teaching and learning skillful ways of being with others in order to build and maintain satisfying relationships. In this chapter, I will offer a model for relationship building based on seven elements, or virtues. If emphasized within ourselves and in our dealings with others, these seven elements will improve the quality of all our personal relationships.

I call this model the Healing Relationship. Over the years, I found that no matter what problems people experienced, no matter what techniques we used to address them, more than anything else, it was the quality of the relationship between client and guide that determined the outcome. A positive result was not dependent on the knowledge of the guide, or the sophistication of the intervention, but rather was dependent on the quality of the connection.

The reason for this is simple. The person or group experiencing the difficulty, not the guide, must do the work to ameliorate it. Nothing a second party does can remove the client's impediment. What the guide can do is provide a context in which the client feels motivated, energized, and safe enough to open to the critical insights that allow for healing and make possible the necessary changes.

It became clear that what was within my control as a guide, what worked to facilitate life affirming shifts in the lives of others, was to maintain an attitude that supports and empowers the other. My attitude— expressed through words, body language and behavior— when experienced as respect and support by the client, enhances the possibility that the client will allow positive changes to emerge. It creates a context in which they can let go of the habits of personality that bind them to dysfunctional behavior so they can realize their natural state of emotional health.

Gradually, I discerned the specific elements that constitute the Healing Relationship: the seven elements or virtues and their power to positively influence the quality of relationships. These same elements apply to building and maintaining all types of relationships. I discovered their wide application when I carried them from the professional arena into my family, work, and friendships. My relationships grew richer, deeper, and more satisfying. They brought me more pleasure than ever before.

The purpose of the Healing Relationship is emotional and spiritual growth for ourselves and those we interact with. The primary characteristic of the Healing Relationship is depth—depth of feeling and depth of connection. We go deep within ourselves to harvest our highest virtues and connect with others from that place.

The Seven Virtues of the Healing Relationship

FITTINGLY, AS JUPITER was the most powerful diety in the Roman pantheon, he was the protector of Virtue. The following are the key elements, or virtues, in the Healing Relationship Model:

1. Awareness
2. Truth
3. Acceptance
4. Expression
5. Intuition
6 Intention
7. Nonattachement to outcome

The sequencing of elements unfolds with a developmental logic.

**AWARENESS->TRUTH->ACCEPTANCE->EXPRESSION->
INTUITION->INTENTION ->NON ATTACHMENT**

The seven virtues can be grouped into the three basic components of a healing attitude: 1. *Owning*; 2. *Sharing*; and 3. *Context for Action.*

The first three elements (Awareness, Truth, and Acceptance) constitute the *Owning* component of the Healing Relationship. Owning means to take responsibility for one's own truth and feelings. It is a healthy alternative to our habitual tendency toward judgment and blame of others, and the denial of our own truth.

The fourth virtue (Expression) is *Sharing* ourselves by communicating the truth of our thoughts and feelings with others. Sharing our inner experience, perhaps more than any other single factor, creates intimacy between people. Those we share with feel we have bestowed the gift of ourselves upon them, and through knowing us better are more willing to receive us with warmth and welcome.

The final three virtues (Intuition, Intention and Nonattachment) are the *Context for Action*. Together, these elements create the conditions under which our behavior becomes more skillful, effective, and supportive of ourselves and others.

Let's now examine each of the seven elements in greater depth.

Owning

First, there must be *awareness*. Before anything else, we need to be observant of what is actually happening in the internal and external environment. We need to be aware of ourselves, others, and what is happening between us before real connection takes place.

Secondly, it is necessary to recognize the *truth* about the moment we are sharing with another. The reality of what is happening in the present, untainted as much as is possible by our desire, clinging, or rejection. Seeing what is simply so within me and between us. Otherwise, we are operating with false information in the Never-Never Land of how we want it to be, rather than how it is.

We then need to *accept* the truth of what is, whether we like it or not. Pleasant or unpleasant, we need to accept the truth of the moment. If we reject it or deny it, it becomes more and more difficult to build a healing relationship

Sharing

EXPRESSION IS SIGNIFICANT because after seeing and accepting the truth within and without, the communication of that truth deepens our relationships. It releases tension for the individual doing the expressing and helps us be more present for the interaction. Expression connects us to the listener by creating the kind of intimacy that comes only through sharing ourselves with them.

Context for Action

INTUITION IS OUR GREATEST resource for moving toward skillful action. Building on the owning and sharing virtues, intuition becomes our best guide for effective behavior. From intuition emerges understanding and guidance for our next appropriate steps.

Intention defines and points us in the direction we wish to go. Intention is important because it generates the power of purpose. In relationships, intention demands that we come to agreement about shared goals, and this shared purpose maximizes the potential to achieve them together. Without intention, we may wander about the countryside never arriving at our destination.

Nonattachment is the paradoxical element in the Healing Relationship model. It is also essential to any success we may hope for.

The first six virtues set up the possibility of satisfying relationship. The seventh, an attitude of non-attachment, requires that we do not cling to that outcome. We remain open to all possibilities, accepting all outcomes as permissible, without struggling and squeezing anything into submission.

The ability to be open to outcome, the willingness to accept what is, does not constitute a lack of caring. Rather, it is simple humility. It is the acknowledgment of the truth that we are not in control of the universe and we are wise enough to gratefully receive whatever it brings us. The core of the non-attachment paradox is that it creates the highest probability that the outcome we desire will in fact happen. It is "giving up to get our way." Nonattachment is a highly evolved stance which requires considerable practice to embody in our lives.

All seven virtues need to be operative to live the Healing Relationship. First, within and then in relationship to others. We cannot successfully apply principles to relationships with others that we do not first apply to our relationship with ourselves.

Living the seven virtues creates a powerful quality called *presence*. Presence is projected by one's bearing and results in others feeling comfort and safety in our company. It brings out the very best in others. Presence is a quality that can not be captured in words but which we have all experienced in the fellowship of special people.

To turn an aphorism on its head, "Virtue is *more* than its own reward." I do not advocate cultivating these seven attitudes because they are good, moral, or right. I advocate them because they work. They are wonderful allies in constructing a harmonious balanced life. They help us build strong satisfying relationships and the deep fulfilling connections we so desire.

Of course, we can deceive people and put on a show to engender temporary closeness. In the long run, however, this strategy inevitably fails. It cannot sustain itself over time. Eventually, the truth bleeds through. The underpainting of pretension becomes visible at the surface. Whatever we gain through manipulation or posing will not last. Even in the short run, because it is not authentic, it will not be seriously satisfying to either party.

The Law of karma, the Law of Cause and Effect, is as real and active a principle in the moral sphere of our physical life as the Law of Gravity. In Western terms it is pronounced with the insight, "As we sow, so shall we reap." Or more colloquially, "Whatever goes around, comes around."

For the most part, sincere action produces sincere reaction. And, insincere action produces insincere reaction. It is universal truth. Emphasizing the seven virtues in our relationship with others will be reflected back to us in the quality of our connectedness with others. Our friends will feel more comfortable in our presence. They will be more open to sharing the truth of their own experience with us, perhaps even feel safe enough to express their deeper feelings. Not always, not necessarily of course, but in the long run it will deepen, enrich and enliven our relationships as a whole.

I have seen the magic of the seven virtues in building relationships in a variety of diverse settings. I have seen its effectiveness not only in personal relationships and group settings, but in large complex organizations also.

Business organizations that have had a history of mistrust between labor and management can become cooperative communities through the activity of Healing Relationship principles. When I have worked with organizations, everyone begins with a suspicion of me, the outsider. If I come with integrity, if I abide by the seven virtues of the healing relationship model, over time connection and trust build. People move from mistrust to respect, sometimes even affection. Ultimately they transfer that style of relating to each other and the organization becomes a "kinder and gentler" environment. This evolution comes not from any skills or wisdom I bring, but from the power of the seven virtues and the authority it projects.

A Field of Love

SURROUNDING THE SEVEN VIRTUES like a field within which they flourish is the quality of love. Love provides the context for the Healing Relationship because it is the fundamental connecting agent in the universe. Bringing love to the field creates an atmosphere in which relationships flourish and healing occurs. Love is the *being state* in which the *doing* of the virtues happens. Love is the ground from which the other elements spring—it implies and includes them all. And, when the seven virtues are active, love is further built and strengthened.

Love is the essential energy of the God-principle. Love is the palpable vibration of Essence in the physical world. When we feel love, we are in touch with Essence. As Martin Luther said, "Love is an image of God, and not a lifeless image. It is the living essence of Divine nature."

Love is demonstrated to another primarily through the attitude and behavior of Acceptance. Acceptance is experienced as unqualified positive regard. No matter what I am doing, or have done, when you accept me, I feel loved. Acceptance recognizes the divine identity of the other no matter how deeply buried or hidden it is at any given moment. Love knows the true nature of the other despite the chinks in personality that are inevitable and visible.

The sense of being loved for who we are without conditions or coercion, though silent, comes through at high volume like the beauty of a Chopin symphony. It is powerfully received and felt. Acceptance and love are the most powerful agents of connecting and healing we know.

The "how to" of loving is simple in concept yet difficult in execution. It can be seen as a two-part process. The primary step is to remember our own identity as Essence and drop into the feeling state associated with experiencing ourselves in that way. Secondly, we remember that whatever is going on at the surface level with the other person, beneath that is their true identity as Essence. Holding that definition of the other, while interacting with them, allows the full expression of love.

This kind of love is not romantic love and it is not something you "fall into." The concept of "falling in love," like the image it embodies, implies a process of descending into a psychological experience. The love we are referring to is about ascending into Spirit. For all the heat, fire, and joy of romantic love, it is mostly a powerful projection process. It begins as a light projection in which we see in the other qualities we admire and have ourselves but do not manifest. We are attracted to the light of those qualities, to the missing love for ourselves, and therefore to the person manifesting our light, with the intensity of the moth drawn to a flame.

As we all know, romantic love is both wonderful and terrible. It embodies the thrills of a roller coaster, with all its highs and lows. Romantic love happens to us because we reside in these human personalities and cannot help but launch projections.

Spiritual love does not just happen to us, it must be consciously cultivated. If we do not ground romantic attraction into a larger spiritual context, the romantic experience will eventually run to the other side, the shadow projection process. Aversion will emerge with the same intensity as the original attraction.

When we understand that real Love is not romantic love or projection, but divine energy emerging as felt experience, then our relationships become more harmonious and balanced.

What needs our attention, work and focus is the cultivation of divine love. We are addressing the classic distinction between *eros* and *agape*. Eros is love at the personality level. Agape is God-energy manifested at the human level. Agape is love at the depth of Essence. Agape facilitates healing long lasting satisfying relationship.

There is a beautiful true story about the Tibetan refugee community in India told by the Dali Lama's sister. After the Chinese invaded and took control of Tibet, many Tibetans fled persecution and established a community in exile at Dharmasala, India. The first groups that arrived recreated the norms of loving kindness that are inherent in Tibetan Buddhist culture. During the initial period of inception and for many years afterwards, the community was marked by peace and harmony.

More recently, however, young refugees arrived who did not grow up in the Tibetan Buddhist culture of loving kindness, but have lived their entire lives under the brutal and repressive colonial rule of the Chinese. These young people arrived to Dharmasala emotionally wounded and with a great deal of pain and anger. Many have "acted out" intensely, sometimes through crime and violence.

As the problem of these young arrivals escalated and became recognized, the community gathered to address it. After considering various options, they moved toward the solution most natural to them — one they knew would build healing. More love. How different from our "get tough on crime" response, which has been spectacularly unsuccessful in positively influencing youth.

The community recommitted itself to being more loving to these youths through offering unconditional acceptance and support. The Dali Lama's sister reported that within three months of this recommitment, the violent behavior dropped away. The young people grew into peaceful members of a serene community and living examples of the healing power of love.

Exercise

The healing power of love operates at all levels of the human experience: self, relationship, and community. You can find evidence of this in your own life. Remember a time you had a healing experience. Was love at the center?

Remember a time you experienced healing in a relationship. Was love at the center?

Remember a time you experienced healing in a family or community. Was love at the center?

The experience of love in our lives bears out the truth that love is the field within which healing and relationship grow.

Awareness

AWARENESS IS THE ground of the Healing Relationship. It callS for us to be aware of the unfolding of present events, both within our self and in the external world. Awareness is bare attention to what is in the moment, as it is unfolding. Though fundamental and profoundly basic, awareness is challenging to develop.

Attention naturally oscillates between thought, feeling, and sensation, then returning to awareness of the present. When we begin to pay close attention to the nature of our awareness, it becomes apparent that most of the time we are lost in thought. We are usually attending to past and future, worry and planning, not the bare truth of the now. Our attention is unmindful of the present. The present unfolds while our attention is elsewhere. It is focused on the movie playing in our mind. Our overall level of true awareness of the internal and external present is generally low.

The problem created by lack of awareness is that when our attention is elsewhere, we are blind to the truth of what is so right now. It is ignorance at its most basic level. We don't know what is happening because we are not present for it. It is as if experience and relationship are happening outside the theater we are seated in. We are in the dark, watching a different movie.

In the presence of another person, this lack of "being there" is strikingly apparent. It is experienced and felt as a lack of concern and caring. We feel diminished and slightly abandoned. Being present through awareness is fundamental to satisfactory relationships.

Awareness is characterized by receptivity; it is open and receiving to the present. When our mind is in a state of awareness, it is not wandering to the past or future, nor is it planning or worrying.

The Buddhists teach that the highest function of mind is not thought but awareness. As culturally conditioned beings, however, we are not well trained in using the mind for that function. We are conditioned to use it mainly for thought. This is one of the reasons that Nature strikes such a deep chord in us and is so satisfying. The awe-inspiring wonder of natural beauty demands attention. It pulls the mind out of its conditioned state into bare attention. This unfettered state of pure awareness provides rest and relief from the ramblings of ideas and worry.

Exercise

Reeducating the mind is a necessary first step for shifting its use towards bare attention. Meditation is the most effective vehicle with which to retrain ourselves in order to make this shift. In Vipassana Buddhism, meditation is called "mindfulness practice." The mechanism is simple. With eyes closed and the body quiet, we bring our attention to the breath. Without changing its natural rhythm, we notice and focus exclusively on the movement of the breath, as it comes in and goes out. When we notice that the attention has wandered from the breath, without judgment or blame, we gently return it to focused attention on the breath.

The insights revealed to us by this simple practice of observation, about how our mind works, is invaluable. The practice also trains the mind into the habit of returning to bare awareness once we have noticed that it has wandered from the present. You will observe, if you do this mediation experiment, that most of the time awareness is not on the breath. It is attending to thought, feeling, or physical sensation. It generally takes quite a while before we even notice that we have wandered from the present. We are lost in thought, without the awareness that we are thinking. Most of the time our mental process is more like a waking dream than a consciously chosen activity.

Without the experience of observing the movement of the mind, most of us mistakenly believe that our awareness is attending the present, and that we choose where we put our attention. Experience in observing the mind, however, demonstrates a different reality. The truth is we have too little clear awareness of what is going on inside or outside of us. We spend most of our conscious time floating in this waking dream. Further, we are unconscious that we are even dwelling in this dream state, until something or someone wakes us from it. Only then do we notice, after the fact, where our attention has been.

It is important to practice cultivating awareness through meditation and other techniques, because awareness will not grow on its own, or simply because we will it. Unfortunately, our "awareness muscle" has become flaccid and needs work. It requires training to bring it back to fitness. When once again fit, the mind can be quick to notice that attention has wandered from the present, and provide us the choice to return to the now, or stay with the float of our waking dream.

Cultivating awareness is life transforming. It revolutionizes our ability to thoroughly experience the present and to be fully available for it. Awareness is the primary component of what we call "presence," that subtle but powerful quality of fully "being there" for the moment, for the other, and for relationship. Presence is so strongly projected and received that through it we can share and experience intimately the present together.

Presence constitutes true integrity. The other person feels this integrity as an as honoring of who they are. We are fully with them in both the giving and receiving. This total "thereness," as against a limited and partial attendance, builds deeply satisfying and enduring connection.

Presence provides an emotional safety net to those with whom we relate because they feel the shelter of our company. They can let loose, take risks and glow in the joy of who they are, with our presence as their support. They experience a sanctuary within which it is possible to more fully feel, open, express, and heal. When one feels safe enough to fully feel and share those feelings with us, even without making actual changes in circumstances, they feel better, and our connection is deepened.

With awareness of the inner process, we experience the truth of what is unfolding within us. We feel the feelings as they are. We avoid the self-ignorance caused by the absence of attention. Through choosing to maintain awareness of our feelings and the insights arising out of them, release and connection happen. We become more available and present to ourselves and those we care about.

Truth is Healing

THE SPIRITUAL TEACHER Joel Goldsmith observes that, "Truth is a synonym for God." Honesty with one's self and others is central to beneficial relationship. We must first be truthful with our self, if we are to be honest with others. When we do not recognize or are not willing to open to what is true in ourselves, we are in denial. We are living in a fantasyscape where it is not possible to be useful to others.

When we do not honor the truth of what is, thoughts and actions become confused. Relationships become cloudy and there is misunderstanding. We may begin to work at cross purposes and stir up conflict in the relationship. In an interesting scene in the film "Beloved Immortal," Beethoven's secretary says aptly, "There is no peace without truth."

Honesty with others, though sometimes very difficult, is critical to the Healing Relationship. As in the children's tale of the "Three Little Pigs," the hardest house to build, the one which requires the most effort, is the one that stands the longest against the onslaughts of the wolf. The relationship built on a foundation of truthfulness and honesty can not be easily knocked over, no matter how much huffing and puffing the world blows our way. Relationships built with straw or sticks, on appearance or falsehoods, will not stand up in the long run.

Nothing kills relationships faster than lies. More relationships have floundered on the rocks of lies than on any other challenge life provides. Not just massive overt lies but accumulated fibs and omissions wreak havoc on relationships. Most importantly, the unwillingness to share the truth in our heart debilitates relationships. The failure to share our truth generates distance, inch by inch, day by day, until an insurmountable chasm opens between us and those we love.

Truth is the awareness of what is and the courage to open to it. Non-truth lacks either awareness or courage. When we are truthful with ourselves and others we are seen in the world as a person of integrity. Joel Goldsmith has said, "Integrity is living your truth." Coming from truth and integrity we are received as sincere and genuine. We are accepted as someone who is neither fearful nor to be feared.

Truth with love generates openness and receptivity in the other. There is no need to defend or hide from us. On the contrary, truth as an example exalts and inspires others to live up to their own genuine selves. People are powerfully attracted by simple authenticity. Deeper connection inevitably results.

Honesty is sometimes hard because it requires the courage to face painful consequences. We are afraid to hurt others with our truth because they may get angry with us. We are afraid they may reject us and we will lose their approval. Truthfulness requires sufficient inner strength so that external approval, while pleasant, is not a necessary element for our survival. We need to learn to cherish high quality relationships more than just any relationship.

Truthfulness with our self may be even harder to swallow. It requires opening to the reality of our unpleasant feelings and desires. We need to be willing to face all of our self and feel all of our feelings: Our anger, our fears, our grief, and our sadness. When we do not accept our inner truth, inevitably it returns to catch us unawares, trips us up and make us fall.

We all must face and conquer the barriers to honoring our inner truth. The fear of feelings, and the fear of loss and disapproval are strong. The fear that if we acknowledge what is true within us, we may be compelled to take actions we do not want. Yet, we all know the exquisite freedom of facing down these demons and living in the full light of truth. When you feel it, it is intoxicating, far beyond the benefit of the small gains generated by denial, deception, or evasion. Truth embodied is the eagle soaring free.

Other obstacles to owning our truth are the moral codes, the shoulds and shouldn'ts we have all grown up with. If we "lust after our neighbors wife," we may deny that painfully obvious reality because it is "wrong." We deny a transparent truth because it is a "should not." First, we deny it to ourselves, and then if necessary to another, resulting in planting a seed in our inner underground which will surely sprout as an unwanted weed. It will spring aggressively forth at a time we least expect it, when we are not ready for it, to disrupt our balance and create havoc in our lives.

If we simply honor the truth of what is, the "suchness" of the feeling, the reality that attraction is there, then it need go no further. No action is required: No breaking of commandants, agreements, or vows. The truth simply is, it does not demand any particular behavior.

We often fail to understand that truth does not require action. It requires awareness. There is truth and we open to it. Nothing more is needed. Our choices for action remain free and unfettered. In fact, it becomes more free and unfettered because nothing is hidden to arise and sabotage our choices.

Knowing that I "lust after my neighbor's wife" is not a demand for action. I am not compelled to infidelity. Similarly, wanting to be rich or famous is not a call to any particular course of behavior in the world of work and finance. We are free to choose our actions. Actions can be chosen, feelings are not. It is better to experience the truth of our feelings and then choose our actions, to lead the life we want, rather than deny the truth and end with a train wreck for a relationship.

Honoring the truth of our feelings allows us to choose our behavior more effectively. It helps us to select actions on the basis of accurate information. Any strategist knows that decisions based on accurate information results in far better outcomes than those predicated on incomplete or incorrect information.

Honoring the truth also releases the energy we must expend to repress the truth. This increase in accessible energy adds vitality and joy to all parts of our lives.

Moving beyond opening to our own truth into sharing it with others is not always necessary. However, whatever challenges honest sharing may present, it inevitably builds deeper connections to the person with whom we share. To talk to your wife about your attraction to your neighbor is less important than knowing the truth that it exists within you. But, finding the courage to talk with her about it, though difficult and upsetting, will inevitably build a stronger more intimate bond between you. Over time, a culture can develop in your relationship in which it is not necessary to deny the truth of who you are. We can learn together to develop the trust that truth is healing and distinct from action, and that the "truth can set us free."

Avoiding truth in our relationships builds walls between people. Some walls may be healthy, but too many form an insurmountable barrier between ourselves and others and cut us off from satisfying connection.

Dishonesty fosters a shared state of delusion that inevitably leads to mutual disappointment. If we allow ourselves to believe something is real when it is not, or something is not real when it is, then the moment that the truth bleeds through and the deception is recognized, it hurts much worse than it would have if originally recognized.

A NECESSARY FACTOR in all positive personal change and growth is the willingness to open to the truth of one's present condition. Sigmund Freud put it accurately when he said simply, "What is suppressed does not heal."

Truth is healing. When combined with speaking that truth, it becomes transformative. Every time we see our inner truth and share it we grow. In groups and organizations, truth-telling is the key to effective cooperative action. Without it, the organization operates at minimal levels of effectiveness. With it excellence is possible.

Employees who know their jobs, but work within a culture of denial and secrecy, get the job done, but at low levels of efficiency relative to their potential. This is the state of most businesses today.

They function and survive, some even prosper, but nowhere near the level of their potential.

Conversely, employees that share truth between them can move mountains. They can probably even make mountains. I have seen this repeatedly in my experience as a workplace consultant. Those organizations whose employees are encouraged to own and share their truth are far more efficient, effective, and profitable than those who do not. A simple depiction of how truth results in organizational effectiveness may be described as follows:

Truth->Trust->Loyalty->Commitment->Excellence.

In India, Mahatma Gandhi lead one of the poorest most disorganized nations on earth to freedom and independence from one of the most powerful and highly organized empires in history. He believed that the single most powerful weapon he had was truth. "Speak truth to evil" he said, and it worked.

The power of truth-telling is apparent in children as well. When mothers are at their end of their tether, filled with frustration, the parental scream often follows. This often scares the wits out of kids. The other day I witnessed a mother of twins, whose nerves were frayed from their incessant demands on her time, react to the final straw of noise making by one of her children. She came charging out of the front door of the house into the yard to confront the twins and give them the full force of her displeasure on high volume. One of the boys, Jimmy, was so frightened by this that he froze in place and started to cry. This pushed Mom's buttons even more, she got red in the face and her voice began to quiver in rage.

The other child, Jonathan, perhaps the more courageous of the two, turned to his mother and said quite simply, "Mommy, when you yell like that it makes me a liddle bit sad and a liddle bit scared." The mother melted. Her entire countenance changed immediately. Her face softened and turned into a smiling glow. She was touched and disarmed by this crystal clear truth spoken by her son. Jonathan was in touch with the truth of his feelings and had the courage to share it. Mom grabbed up both her children and smothered them in kisses.

Acceptance

THE ACTRESS MARGO KIDDER, describing her come back from mental illness, attributed much of her healing to the *acceptance* exhibited by family and friends. She said, "People help other people get well through love and acceptance."

Acceptance is welcoming reception, unconditioned by the need for any prior change in behavior or attitude on the part of the other. We can, of course, better accept others if we learn to accept ourselves. Opening our arms fully and receiving another, just as they are, is made easier if we are able to be gentle, kind, and forgiving to ourselves. Accepting ourselves, whether we like any particular behavior of ours or not, without first requiring a change, is a profoundly healing form of self-love.

To be truly accepting, we need to differentiate the doer from the deed. The doer is always and forever a child of God no matter what he or she does. The deed is an act in the moment, usually coming out of the limited context of personality, which may be constructive, destructive, or neutral. If the behavior is destructive, then it must be seen as such and needs change. The fundamental divinity of the person, however, is not be impugned. We can condemn the behavior but not the person.

Criticism is not the most effective path to change and growth. Criticism wounds and freezes behavior in its dysfunctional state more often than helping to make positive change. Criticism may elicit short run modification in behavior but seldom does it result in long run fundamental change. For healing, growth and connection to occur, unconditional acceptance is peerless.

Acceptance does not mean agreement. Acceptance indicates a belief in the basic worthiness of the other, not in the content of what they say or do. Acceptance assumes that whatever is happening on the surface, at a deeper level there is worthiness.

Many people have returned from the brink of disaster; suicide, crime, prison, addiction and many other forms of darkness through the intervention of acceptance. If just one person believes in us, hope for redemption is alive.

I know a prominent university professor who as a young man was a criminal and a drug addict. Jay did time in San Quentin prison. I asked him one day about this and how his life turned in a more positive direction. He told me that for many years he had been a small-time criminal, living on the edge, and getting away with it. Then one day his luck came to an end. He got busted and sent to prison.

Inside he languished until he met a man named Bill Burdock. Bill's unconditional acceptance turned Jay's life completely around. Bill had been an inmate at San Quentin himself and now as his form of service he came to San Quentin on a weekly basis to visit and help those prisoners who had no one else to support them. Bill took Jay under his wing. He believed in Jay's essential goodness. Bill saw through the exterior trimmings of the petty criminal to the real person underneath, the man worthy and deserving of respect. Bill gave Jay that respect without preconditions.

"He believed in me when I didn't believe in myself," Jay told me. "I figured if Bill thought I was all right, I could think of myself that way too. Through him I learned to accept myself and believe in myself. Everything fell into place after that."

When our true nature is seen by another soul, it helps begin the healing of self-criticism that is so often at the root of failure. When Bill accepted Jay as fundamentally worthy, even though Jay's behavior was not, he built a bond of steel between them. Upon that bond and the self-worth it engendered was constructed a doctorate degree and a distinguished university teaching career. Being received in this way, with gladness and understanding, creates the context for healing and cements connection between persons.

When we are accepted, we know it immediately, we feel it, whether it is spoken or not. Acceptance is experienced in the body as a sense of relief, the dropping of a burden. We no longer feel pressured to convince others that we are okay. All the energy that was previously focused on constructing a personal defense or face for the world can be dropped. A river of energy is released making connections with others a deeper and more joyful event.

For many, acceptance is difficult to cultivate. We have been conditioned to judge and criticize ourselves and others. It is very challenging to change that critical habit and learn to hold positive regard for others as our basic stance.

To let go of judgment is not to become indiscriminate. There is a distinction between judgmental criticism and positive discernment.

Discernment does not need to include negative judgment. If we feel some one's behavior is harmful, or we don't like being in their presence, we use our faculty of discernment to move away from that behavior. We can choose to communicate our dislike of the behavior in a context of love without criticizing who they are. Again, it is a matter of separating the music from the music maker. We can love and honor another's Essence while at the same time move away from their behavior and or communicate our displeasure.

Acceptance is fostered by compassion. It grows through experiencing and acknowledging the truth of our own shortcomings and failures. How often have we messed up and caused pain to ourselves and those around us? Then surely we must accept that reality in others.

"Let he who is without sin throw the first stone." From this recognition we learn that all of us are not only capable of wrongdoing but in fact do err far too often. Having recognized and embraced our own darkness, we have more compassion for the foibles of others.

Acceptance has a powerful impact on relationships because it creates an atmosphere of safety. Acceptance allows me to risk being who I am in a relationship because it is the safety net for the adventure my partner and I committed exploring together.

Intimate relationship — marriage or life partnership — is the great crucible for working on acceptance. Many married couples do not accept each other just as they are. Partners often want to change each other into their image of the ideal spouse. The relationship then becomes a subtle or no-so-subtle effort to influence the other to change, waiting for the shift before acceptance is offered. The change never comes and the suffering of mutual nonacceptance hinders the flourishing of the relationship.

This hoped for change cannot happen because the image of the "ideal spouse" is a projection onto the partner; it is not their natural character. The shift we desire doesn't come and we end up living in disappointment with our life partners.

No one can meet the conditions laid out by our idealized images. The lack of acceptance that follows creates marital unhappiness and pain. Conditional acceptance, which amounts to nonacceptance or rejection, is felt like a blade in the heart, not just painful but often lethal. If we can learn acceptance, the sense of relief, joy, and satisfaction that comes with it is a tonic for healing a strained connection. We begin to appreciate, enjoy, and even cherish the wonderful uniqueness that is our partner.

Self-acceptance and accepting others furthers everyone's ability to reach their maximum potential. It provides firm ground upon which to risk experimentation. It builds the confidence necessary to explore unknown territory.

I have often witnessed the impact on the "bottom line" that the quality of acceptance has in the business setting. When management accepts employees for who they are, rather than offering conditional acceptance based upon an image of how they ought to be, great things happen. Productivity soars and relations between people at all levels improves. Friendship and community replaces animosity and fear. All the popular management theories and trends pale compared to the bottom line power of acceptance.

We can further understand the positive impact of acceptance by looking at its opposites; judgment and blame. Both judgment and blame are usually experienced as attack. They cause the recipient to close and defend, rather than open and welcome.

Judgment and blame hurt the recipient and limit the potential quality of relationship. Acceptance unlocks and heals, paving the way for deeper connection.

THE EXECUTIVE DIRECTOR of a nonprofit organization almost put the whole enterprise out of business because of his habit of judgment and blame. The purpose of the agency was to help poor kids by teaching work skills, provide job training, and job placement. Ed, the executive director, thinking he was doing the right thing, used criticism and blame as his primary motivational tool. He did it so often and so harshly that he created a level of fear and dissatisfaction among staff members that became intolerable. So much negative reaction was generated by the director's style of judgment and blame that the organization became ungovernable.

Staff felt a profound sense of defeat. They appealed directly to the board of directors for redress. After some investigation, it became clear to the board that Ed's critical style was the main source of organizational dysfunction. After efforts to help him see this and alter his management style failed, the Board fired him. In their search for a new director they sought a candidate whose leadership style was accepting and respectful. Once hired, the new director quickly put the organization back on track.

IN A SITUATION OF CONFLICT and in times of crisis, acceptance becomes even more important in maintaining relationships. Conflict implies a difference in interests, views or goals. It invariably stimulates the belief that "we are right" and the judgment that "they are wrong."

There is an alternative to the judgmental mind set. We can accept the other even in opposition. "I have this view and you have that." Period. End of story, leaving out the bit about we are right and you are wrong. The difference exists, of course, the conflict is there, we may even see the other's facts or view as "wrong," but we need not judge the other's essential self as wrong. We separate the ideas from the person, rejecting the former while embracing the latter.

Friction is often the result of simple style differences. Two people with different styles rubbing up against each other causes friction. Neither is right, neither is wrong, each is simply different from the other. There are many types of chronic conflicts which are nothing more than clashes of style, no different than you liking sweaters and I like sweatshirts. Orderliness versus disorderliness, for example, is a classic cause of for interpersonal friction. Structure versus lack of structure is another. When these types of opposing orientations bump into each other in a household or office, sparks fly. If we just let them fly, without making the other wrong, the relationship is enlivened not diminished.

In intimate connection, the ability to allow differences without diminishing the other is both challenging and critically important. The happiest couples cherish the other's idiosyncracies because they are a reminder of their beloved's uniqueness. Difference becomes a cause for celebration rather than a bone of contention.

❋ ❋ ❋ ❋ ❋

Exercise

One interesting way to expand your acceptance of others, is to experience the world as they experience it. How, from the perspective of the other, do things fit together and makes sense?

A playful way to experiment with this is to mimic another person's body language. All the emotions are reflected in the body. The way in which a person holds herself is a reflection of the way she is experiencing the moment. If you hold yourself in the same way, you will experience a taste of the feelings she is experiencing. Life from inside her moccasins.

When you see you are not accepting another person, when you feel judgmental, stop for a moment, and try this experiment. Let go of the criticism and unobtrusively adapt the most obvious aspects of their body posture. Put your body into the same position and configuration. Now, focus on your own feelings in this posture and empathetically notice what insights arise for you about how they are experiencing the world.

For example, if the other's head is leaning to the right and their left palm is curled up on their lap, do the same with your head and palm. Then, really drop into what you feel like in this posture. Let the feeling holding that posture be all your are experiencing and let insights arise as to what viewpoint that feeling generates.

More likely than not, insights will come up which will open your understanding of their viewpoint. You will find yourself more accepting. Notice how much better it feels to be accepting rather than judgmental. Notice how it results in relationship building rather than destruction.

I love the biblical phrase, "Judge not that ye may not be judged." If we took this injunction seriously, there would be deep healing and much more satisfying relationship in our lives.

CHAPTER TEN

The Healing & Processing Relationship

Just as a person is drawn by the artist,
surroundings are created by the activity of the mind.
The Buddha

We vote for reality with our imagination.
Carolyn Casey

Expression

EXPRESSION IS THE communication element in the Healing Relationship model. Expression bridges the inner experience to the outer experience. Nothing builds relationship more effectively than the process of sharing.

Expression is also fundamental to the healing process because it is the primary vehicle for emotional release. In one sense, expression literally means release, as in "expressing a wound" indicates releasing waste material from an injury.

Expression lies at the intersection of the internal and external experience. It marks the beginning of the evolution of the internal process of awareness, truth, and acceptance into external action.

We sometimes express our internal state inaccurately because of our conditioning to try and control the environment to make it safe. We may say things that make us look good in order to get approval or avoid pain, rather than express our inner truth. This is a survival mechanism that grew into fixed habit because it helped us take care of ourselves as powerless children. As adults, however, it is no longer an effective strategy. Attempting to control our environment by portraying an image we believe will be acceptable to others can, in fact, be quite harmful. It alienates us from ourselves, distances our actions from our truth, and eats away at our self-respect. It diminishes the very relationship we are trying to control because it builds an inherently weak counterfeit connection that will not hold up under pressure.

Expressing our truth, just as it is, without editorial attempts to control the listener's response is incredibly liberating and healing. Honoring the truth of our inner state, accepting it, and expressing it fully has a restorative affect.

❋ ❋ ❋ ❋ ❋

Excercise

To experience this for yourself, recall a feeling that has been disturbing you. For example, you may be jealous of a friend's success in business. Open to that truth and fully accept it without self-judgment or criticism. Just say to yourself, "I am jealous, and that's the way it is." Say it again, a few times slowly and let it sink in. Now notice how you feel. Is there a sense of relief, a dropping of tension, a smile curling on your lips? Have the disturbing feelings themselves diminished?

❋ ❋ ❋ ❋ ❋

There is power in expression, even without change in circumstances. It produces inner harmony and outer balance.

There are many forms of expression besides verbal that create healing and connection. Keeping a journal, writing poetry, fiction, or nonfiction all help us clarify our thoughts and release feelings onto the page. Writing your feelings in a letter to someone with whom you are having difficulty, with or without sending it, is a wonderful way to discharge the pressure in the relationship.

The writing process clarifies your thoughts, gives you a better understanding of what you are feeling, cools down your sense of conflict, and gives you the confidence that comes with focus.

Recently, my partner Barbara and I had a dandy of a fight. Eventually, we got fed up with going around in word circles and just stopped. I went out to my studio and began to write. I wasn't quite sure what I wanted to do and then remembered a technique that a friend of mine, David Isaacs, told me about to clarify confusion. You ask yourself questions on the written page in "UPPER CASE" letters and then allow the answers to flow spontaneously out in "lower case" letters. I had never done this before, but lacking a better alternative I gave it a try.

The result was amazing. So much clarity emerged. New and helpful information came pouring out of me onto the written page from its previously not-yet-conscious home. By spontaneously responding in writing to my self-directed questions, without the intervention of thought or censoring, I learned why I felt hurt so often in relationships. I was ready to change that habit.

THROUGH THE WRITING process I saw how the feelings I was experiencing, which I thought were particular to the topic and person I was fighting with, was really an old and deeply ingrained pattern. It had little to do with Barbara or the content of our disagreement. It was rooted in my personal history.

As a child, I was hurt by the overly harsh words of adults around me whom I loved. When those tones arise in my adult life with people I am close to, the same old crusty feelings are revived. As I did then, I do now. I use one of the few protective devices available to children: I withdraw to safeguard myself and punish the other with my absence. The understanding that this old pattern was the source of my present frustration was a revelation and arose directly out of the writing exercise. It gave me the insight I needed to drop this debilitating habit and begin to heal.

Writing out my feelings lead me to the causal level, where the problem originated. Now it was potentially solvable. At the symptom level—the content of the argument with Barb—it cannot be solved. At the argument level, we are just chasing our tales. That is why so many arguments go round in circles, ending only in the diminishment of the quality of the relationship.

There are many forms of the expressive arts that can help us find healing and connection through expression. Drawing, painting, and sculpting all can produce healing experiences. Using these expressive arts as a starting point for sharing our inner life helps build and strengthen our relationships.

Physical expression: Dance, sport, and movement of any kind are allies in the healing and connecting process. The release derived from movement and exertion is direct and affirmative. Blocked and stored energy is dissipated quickly. The body reestablishes equilibrium and receptivity. I often run, bike, or do weight training when I feel emotionally constricted. Invariably, the physical expression releases the stuck energy and I am sufficiently refreshed to have a new and more positive perspective on what previously had me stuck.

Expression builds upon awareness, truth, and acceptance. It is the second stage, or booster rocket component, of the Healing Relationship. When we notice the source of an inner feeling and accept its truth, healing and connection begin. When we take it to the next level and express it, share it, the process is expanded substantially.

THE OTHER DAY I was having a conversation with Barbara when an image of a shopping mall popped into my head, seemingly "out of nowhere." It had a dreamlike quality. So, I took a quiet moment to treat it as a dream, dropping into the image and noting the feelings it evoked. I remembered going shopping with my mother as a kid. In those days she would drag me along shopping with her and I hated it. But I remembered a time when we were standing together at a bus stop waiting to go home from such an expedition. I asked her to teach me one of her skills that I had always admired. Gum cracking. It seemed a magical performance, to make that giant noise with just gum.

There we were—I saw it in my mind's eye—my mother and I at the bus stop, her teaching me how to crack gum. She demonstrated how to chew the gum until it became pliable, how to position it between my back teeth, and how to bite down just so, to make it "crack." I remembered vividly the joy of success I felt when I was able to make that first sharp noise with the gum. I was proud and we shared that moment of triumph.

It was wonderful to relive the memory. When I came out of my reverie and shared it with Barbara, it was even richer. Through expressing it, I realized that image was "called up" because it echoed the simple joy Barbara and I were having in that moment together. Expressing it to her deepened the precious quality of our appreciation for each other and our loving connection.

AS WE ALL KNOW, some truths are harder to express than others. Those declarations which we think will offend someone else, hurt, or anger them are especially difficult. This has been a challenge for me all my life. Saying something I feared would upset another has been bound up in my youthful experience of being punished for saying what was true. The consequences for truth telling were sometimes severe. I learned to be cautious and manipulative about what I said. It kept me safe.

As I moved into adulthood this habit became costly. I paid in the diminished quality of relationships. My reticence to open up and share with people was no longer protecting me but hurting me by limiting the depth of my connections. My lack of willingness to express myself froze relationships at a superficial level. My unexpressed feelings and dissatisfactions lay dormant, and arose as explosions when other issues built up the pressure. Such reactions were out of proportion to the presenting circumstances and made the people around me uncomfortable. I hurt, angered or scared my friends and partners far more than if I had expressed my truth in the moment, as it came up, throughout the relationship.

Will Schutz, the author of *Joy* and *The Truth Option*, describes a continuum of truth telling. The more superficial end of the continuum is the point where we tell the truth about the other: the truth about *you*. The more profound and truthful pole, the more challenging end of the continuum, is telling the truth about *me*. Owning what is true about me and sharing it with you.

If I experience my partner as "controlling," for example, the more superficial truth to express is, "You are controlling." The deeper, more useful and challenging response would be something like, "I feel afraid when I sense I am being controlled." The latter expression is more truthful because it goes to the source of the experience.

It is also more reliably accurate. We know we are feeling controlled and we know it does not feel good. Whether the other person is actually aware of trying to control us is strictly conjecture. "You are controlling" is not necessarily true. "I am afraid" most certainly is.

Secondly, expressing the truth about one's self rather than the other is relationship building. We are sharing who we are with the other and thereby inviting them into our inner world. Conversely, the "truth" about *you* is most often critical and blaming and invites distance through defense or attack.

Schutz's truth continuum describes a line from speaking about the other to speaking about one's self. Speaking the truth about one's self is the most true, the most healing, the most relationship building. In the end, it is also the most liberating.

Expressing Difficult Feelings

OUR DIFFICULT FEELINGS like anger, sadness, and fear tend to be the hardest to express. When we do, however, they open up an avenue for healing, connection, and liberation. Most of us know, for instance, that it is important to share our grief in order to release it. We know it is better to honor rather than bury our sadness in order to get through it. Expressing grief to a trusted listener, gradually relieves our pain and we can progressively open to the joy on the other side of the sadness.

The same principle holds true for fear and anger. After opening to our fear, expressing it is a releasing and healing process. Contrary to our dominant cultural conditioning, the macho ethic supports hiding and burying our fear, expressing it connects and builds relationships.

Anger requires more skill and practice to successfully express and release. If our expression of anger means blowing up in accusation, then it is not relationship building. The usual alternative (suppressing the anger and letting it seethe inside) is also a poor choice. It is unhealthy emotionally and physically, and suppression of anger, sooner or later, fractures relationships. In the moment of suppression a barrier to connection is created. Because unexpressed anger inevitably turns into resentment and eventually leaks out, it can cause those we love great pain and sometimes is the source of violence.

In contrast to suppression, if we open to the feeling of anger within us, allow ourselves to experience it fully, literally feeling the anger without bestowing the hot energy on any outside source, then it can dissipate. It can be completed without hissing out at a later time as venom.

The technique is to completely surrender to the internal experience of anger, feel it as it rises up, peaks, and then subsides. Experiencing the anger fully and privately. If we try to express it before it diminishes internally, the communication may be too "hot."

It works better to express our anger after it has dropped from its peak. Then we can say more calmly, "I'm angry about this and I would like to talk about it." Such an invitation is an opening to deepen the relationship rather than fracture it.

However we express our anger, telling the truth about our fundamental feelings requires courage. Sometimes we just need to be willing to accept unpleasant, short-term reactions and consequences for the benefit of the long-term outcome. The willingness to accept a temporary discomfort for an extended gain is a hallmark of the mature relationship.

Courage is not the absence of fear. Courage is the willingness to do the right thing in the face of fear. The World War II hero General George Patton said, "Courage is fear holding out a minute longer."

Another block to expressing our truth originates with how we are socialized as children. We are mistakenly taught that if we feel and express a desire, it demands action. In fact, once we are aware and accepting of our inner truth, then expressing it at the appropriate time and place can free us from the compulsion to act it out. Expression diminishes the likelihood of behaving destructively or in a way that goes against our moral code. Expression is a safety valve through which we can release energy that may otherwise be released through action.

Carl Rogers, the father of Humanistic Psychology, constructed a formula that integrates the elements of the Healing Relationship into a model for effective communication. Roger's says that authentic communication, the hallmark of a satisfying relationship, is based on the concept of "congruence." For authentic communication to be present there must be congruence, or consistency, at three different levels.

The first and deepest level, our fundamental feelings and thoughts, must be congruent with the second level, our awareness and willingness to accept those thoughts and feelings as true. That is to say, we must not to kid ourselves about our inner experience, even if it does not fit with our image of who we would like to be. The third and last level is expression: bridging from what we know is true about ourselves to communicating that truth to others. If we are truthful at all three levels we are congruent. When we are congruent, we are more healthy, balanced, and harmonious because internal conflict has been eliminated.

Real expression is full expression of our inner experience. Not partial communication or the superficial "you" end of the continuum. Not just the parts we think others will like or approve of, but communication of our full truth—warts and all.

Over time cultures have developed aids to facilitate truthful expression. The talking staff, for example, used by aboriginal peoples all over the world, encourages truth telling in the relationship and community context. The talking staff is a device used by two or more people to help them go within themselves to discover their genuine truth and share it. The guideline in using the staff is that the person holding the staff speaks and the others listen without comment. The process is non-interactive, and the speaker knows that she or he need not construct their comments to withstand the criticism of others. It helps the person speaking feel at ease, safe, and confident, devoting his or herself to expression without concern for protection or defense. The speaker is free to concentrate fully on discovering what is within and then sharing it.

This form of expression allows the listener to be released from the job of evaluating and composing a response. The listener can devote full attention to the speaker and thereby receive the message in its entirety.

Because the expression that results from talking staff communication is so deeply truthful and profoundly real, it takes on a sacred quality. There is silence, empathy, laughter, and tears. The talking circle becomes a place of boundless healing and connection.

Exercise

Try the following exercise as a way of experimenting with different pathways to expression. Get in touch with a strong feeling you are experiencing or have experienced in the recent past. It can be a happy feeling or an uncomfortable emotion. Drop into it and without active thinking simply encounter the feeling. Let it be all that is going on for you.

Now, draw the feeling. Express it through the free and uninhibited use of color and line. Without any effort to create something good, pretty, or artistic, download the feeling from the inside to the outside by putting color and line onto paper. Now, study the drawing and write down words that come to you spontaneously that describe it. For example "vivid," "dark," "circle," etc. Write whatever words come without thinking or censoring. Don't try to "get it right," just use the words that flow out spontaneously.

Now, link these words, adding any others that naturally arise, and create a poem. Again, freely and easily, without any effort to write artistic or beautiful verse, express your self.

When your poem is on the page, you can even turn it into a song. Sing it or dance it—any expression that pleases you.

Finally, share whatever piece of this process you care to with someone you trust. Feel the satisfaction of full expression, notice the wonderful release it provides, and notice the way it connects you more deeply to the person with whom you are sharing.

Intuition

IN CHAPTER 8, I covered the role of intuition in our quest for a balanced life. Here, I will describe how intuition serves as the next virtue in the Healing Relationship, recalling some of the key points from our earlier discussion.

Having opened our awareness, accepted the truth of the moment and expressed it, intuition is the next virtue in the Healing Relationship and the first element in the bridge to effective action. Intuition, the sense of inner knowing, is our best ally in constructing behavior. Quieting ourselves and listening to "the still small voice," guides us toward the next best step in healing and relationship building.

To make use of the power of intuition, we need to emphasize the quality of receptivity. For intuition to come alive within us, we need to experiment with relaxing the need for control. It will soon become a relief and pleasure to grow the intuitive process, loosening the domination of the planning and worrying mind and allowing our inner brilliance to easily and naturally produce effective guidance.

The intuitive process provides a pathway for the unconscious mind to become accessible, to communicate, with the conscious mind. This communication comes in the form of a inner guidance. For many, intuition comes as the still small voice, for some as visual images, and for others as an overall feeling or sense of knowing. Whatever the form, intuition is the messenger of integrated and synthetic information that can serve us as a most reliable ally.

Having been guided by the first four steps in the Healing Relationship, intuition requires only that we become quiet and receive its direction. This is a simple process, but it requires the difficult work of breaking our long standing habit of trying to figure everything out with the analytical mind. We are so accustomed to mental struggle and idea wrestling that it is hard for us to simply receive the brilliance that is there for the taking.

In his brilliant book the *Tao of Leadership*, John Heider offers us some guidelines on how to adopt intuition into our relationships:

> When you cannot see what is happening . . . , do not stare harder.
> Relax and look gently with your inner eye.

When you do not understand what a person is saying, do not grasp for every word. Give up you efforts. Become silent and listen with your deepest self.

When you are puzzled by what you see or hear, do not strive to figure things out. Stand back for a moment and become calm. When a person is calm, complex events appear simple.

To know what is happening, push less, open out, and be aware. See without striving. Listen quietly rather than listening hard. Use intuition and reflection rather than trying to figure things out.

The more you can let go of trying and the more receptive you become, the more easily you will know what is happening.

Some people know the value of intuition, but most of us have been directed away from it and are unaccustomed to accessing this side of our self. The intuitive faculty has not been valued in our culture.

Yet we can prove to ourselves the value of the intuitive process by using the holy grail of the western mind, the scientific or experimental method. In this case, use your self as the subject. With an experimental attitude of critical observation, test the outcome of intuition. Use it and see if it works. Begin slowly, using intuition to guide your actions in small matters and collect data as you go. If your intuitive voice guides you well it will build confidence in the process as you prove its validity.

Beginning the experiment simply, start with modest matters using intuition to decide what to order from the menu or what movie to go to, and then notice if we are happy with our choice. Then work up to bigger issues like what kind of car to buy or whether to switch jobs. If your intuitive guidance continues to provide reliable direction, you gain certainty that intuition is an ally in all matters great and small.

The voice of intuition can be recognized and differentiated from other internal chatter by the feeling, tone, and qualities associated with it. Intuition communicates gently, quietly, and always with a positive and supportive intention. Inner voices and direction that do not have these qualities are not intuition. Voices that are harsh or critical are likely to be communication from unhealed sub-personalities. They are calls for healing not the mechanism of guidance. The voice of intuition is "still" and "small" and speaks to us kindly and gently like a loving parent.

Continue to hold the scientific attitude of observation, noting the outcome of your experiments each time, and fine tune your methodology as you go. Use the data of your experiment to determine the fruitfulness of this tool and the proper methodologies that suit your instincts. As Carolyn Casey says, "Believe nothing, entertain everything."

I have observed how the intuitive style often dominates the approach of people we generally think of as the most logic-based, analytical group in our society: computer wizards. Watching programmers and analysts in different challenging situations, I notice how they often follow inner direction more than logic for guidance. They get into a rhythm, trusting their intuition and following its flow, continually risking, experimenting, observing, adjusting and learning. Their confidence builds, and after awhile they seem to be willing to take even bigger risks because their confidence in their inner guidance is so strong.

In the Healing Relationship, intuition is the wisdom of the Center. It is the tool behind the tools. It provides stability and direction in the stormy seas of emotion and intellect. Interacting from intuition ensures that we are connecting with another soul from a place of mutual interest because the relationship will emerge from a source common to both—Essence.

Intention

INTENTION FOCUSES INTUITION into skillful action by providing the target towards which we can aim our behavior. By defining our goals and focusing our action, intention empowers us as participants in the creation of our own reality. Adding clarity of purpose to our behavior, we increase the likelihood of achieving the desired outcome.

Often, our hopes and dreams remain amorphous. When they are unformed in this way, it is difficult to construct and link the individual elements of our behavior into action strategies that produce the desired results. Once we clarify and focus formless desires into specific intentions, we are more likely to hit the mark because we know where to aim.

Because of its power to manifest outcome, intention is important in the Healing Relationship. In medicine, intention literally means, "The process by which, or the manner in which, a wound heals."

Intention is important to success at the beginning and throughout the life of an action or enterprise. At the beginning, intention is critical because it defines the destination. We know where we are going so we can construct a route that will take us there. It is difficult to go from San Francisco to Los Angeles if we do not know we want to go to Los Angeles. It is the defined intention to go to Los Angeles that allows us to map an effective route and follow it there.

Intention continues to be important all along the way. Other roads and roadblocks will inevitably appear during our journey. Enticements and detours will arise. We can become lost in these diversions, forget where we are going, and begin to think that the diversions are the destination. Without keeping our intention in mind, we can easily get lost.

The saying, "Keep your eyes on the prize," is an excellent guideline. It reminds us of the importance of intention. Keeping our eyes on the prize all along the journey serves as a counter balance to the tendency to get lost in the diversions and forget the destination. Intention becomes more useful and important as the aspirations become more complex and difficult to achieve. It provides motivational power to continue in the face of impediment, disappointment, and setbacks. An absence of intention allows energy to seep out, leaving us with insufficient focus to achieve a difficult end. Intention lines our energy up behind one clearly defined goal, giving us the incisive power of the arrow.

In intimate relationships, agreeing on intention helps partners experience their interpersonal difficulties with a greater sense of perspective. If we agree on our destination, then we can better weather the storm of disagreement around the details of how we get there. If we share the intention to create a beautiful house, for example, we can work through our disagreements about the color scheme for the interior. If we have no clear shared intention, however, or if we forget it along the way, the disagreement becomes an end in itself and both the house and the relationship suffer.

AT THE ORGANIZATIONAL LEVEL, intention is paramount. In complex human systems, it is critical that intention is clearly defined and agreed upon if a many-headed creature like an organization is to pull in one direction and succeed. To at least a modest extent, everyone needs to have the same basic intention in order to generate a purposeful hub around which the wheel of organization can turn.

The single most important element in organizational success is clarity and agreement about intention. In the language of modern business practice it is called "vision." Having a clearly defined and agreed upon vision, the function of the company and its relationship to the marketplace becomes clear. All actions can be aligned to serve that function and nourish the success of the enterprise.

New opportunities for growth that are aligned with the company's vision can be vigorously pursued with a reasonable expectation of success. Those that are not in line with the vision must be discarded, no matter how appealing. Endeavors outside the scope of the central vision will inevitably fail.

On a larger scale, the nation has learned the hard way the importance of Vision. Besides all the other terrible things that emerged from the Vietnam War, it was a debacle from a military perspective because it lacked clear intention. There were hundreds of competing agendas and no unified purpose. As a result, thousands of people died for a war we could never win. We couldn't win because we never defined what winning was.

In contrast, the Gulf War, whatever its political and social shortcomings, had a clearly defined intention from a military perspective. As a military operation it was a success in large part due to the power and advantage at all levels wrought by singularity of purpose. As the ancient Roman's put it, "Where there is unity, there is victory."

At the societal level, intention, or shared vision, is fundamental to the maintenance of an organized, progressive society. One of the wonders of this country is its Constitution and Bill of Rights. These documents not only define our process of governance, but define our intentions as a nation. The power of that vision has supported, protected, and guided us through many difficult challenges. Without it, we could not have maintained the democratic institutions we have preserved and grown. Intention helps generate the resolution and determination necessary to maintain positive social structure. It has been known since the time of the Book of Proverbs, "Where there is no vision, the people perish."

One of the most important contributions of the New Age movement has been the dissemination of the principle that thought is power. Thought is the mechanism that drives outcome. Intention manifests results. As the Buddha said, "Just as a picture is drawn by the artist, surroundings are created by the activities of the mind."

If we think something, we increase our ability to make that something happen. If we do not have a vision of it, or the intention to manifest it, whatever happens is simply the unfolding of events. Intention empowers us and makes us active participants in the creation of our own reality. Carolyn Casey puts it poetically when she says , "We vote for reality with our imagination

There are many examples of how thought or intention creates outcome. All of us have experienced it in our lives. When we are clear about what we want, even though the goal seems difficult and the obstacles many, we can achieve it with the power of intentionality. Many have overcome what physicians have told them were incurable diseases through the power of mind and commitment. I have experienced these transformations in my own life and seen it in the life of others.

I have found the power of intention to heal and build relationship incredibly effective in my own life. I had quite severe back pain for twenty five years due to a lifting injury. Over all that time, though I had not succeeded, I never relinquished the intention to heal my back.

About five years ago, I realized I wasn't going to achieve my goal unless I developed a "healing relationship" with a health practitioner and worked cooperatively to cure my back. I did my research and identified a chiropractor who had success with cases like mine. I began seeing him and explained my intention to have a healthy back. I was committed to doing whatever it took to get strong enough to run and exercise again. I explained that I wanted to enter into a partnership with him to achieve this goal. He was inspired and I was inspired and we went forward.

The doctor took x-rays and told me I had two herniated discs, and that running on a regular basis was unlikely. The only people he had seen come back from this type of injury to run, without an operation, were people who did sufficient weight training to develop the back and abdominal muscle and compensate for the weakness caused by the injured discs. But, he added, he didn't think that type of therapy was appropriate yet, as it might be more injurious than helpful.

I saw the doctor once a week for three months. He gave me exercises to improve my muscle strength and stretches to help the elasticity of the ligaments. He did therapeutic manipulations on my back to realign the skeletal structure. My back progressively improved.

Two months later I stopped into my local gym to check out weight training. The manager welcomed me and when I told him about my back he showed me some exercises that would help me strengthen and align my back muscles without straining them further. The most important thing I could do for my back, he said, was increase the strength of my abdominal muscles so that they would serve as a natural girdle, providing support and releasing pressure from the highly stressed back muscles.

My intention to restore and have a healthy back served to initiate, guide, and focus my healing journey to a successful conclusion. After six months of therapy, exercises, and the weight training, I was pain free and able to run again. What a grand victory and delight it was for me the first time I ran on the beach with the sun and wind in my face feeling the exultation of free movement.

LIKE THE PYRAMID OF ELEMENTS described in the beginning of the previous chapter—the "Who, What and How" of the Healing Relationship—a parallel hierarchy is "Intention, Know ledge, and Skills."

At the base, the most important level of the structure, is intention: Clear commitment to the healing or growth of relationship is critical for the desired outcomes to occur.

In the middle of the pyramid is knowledge: The understanding of the principles that create healing and relationship.

At the top of the pyramid, the part most visible to the observer, are the skills and techniques of the practitioner.

Most people misunderstand the hierarchy. Because the behavioral aspects are the most visible, they emphasize learning skills and techniques to improve relationships. "What can I *do* differently to make this connection better?"

More important than technique is understanding the principles of relationship from which skillful behavior flows. And more important than the principles, is the intention that drives the acquisition of knowledge and ultimately effective behavior. It is the intention that supports the entire structure and is the foundation upon which the outcome rests.

The great German poet Goethe described this well when he said:

> Until one is committed
> there is hesitancy, the chance to draw back,
> always ineffectiveness.
>
> Concerning all acts of initiative and creation
> there is one elementary truth
> the ignorance of which kills countless ideas
> and splendid plans:
>
> that the moment one definitely commits oneself
> then Providence moves too.
>
> a whole stream of events issues from the decision
> raising in one's favor all manner
> of unforeseen incidents and meetings
> and material assistance
> which one could not have dreamt
> would have come their way.
>
> Whatever you can do or dream you can, begin it.
> Boldness has genius, power and magic in it.
>
> Begin it now.

There are many ways to grow the habit of commitment and intentionality. First, take the time before entering into a relationship to check in with yourself. Define what you really want and focus your desires into a clear and specific intention. Slow yourself down enough to disengage and focus the camera of your mind from a fuzzy image of outcome to a clear picture of result. Let that clear picture sink in and take hold. Stay with it and let it serve you all the way through the obstacles and diversions that arise along the journey.

To help yourself remember intention over time, find a few words that define and summarize your intention. As a simple example, you may have been getting colds every winter for the past few years and you want to change that this year. Say to yourself, "I want to be cold free all winter." Using this phrase as an affirmation, remember and repeat it from time to time. It will become an unconscious guide for the day to day behavioral choices necessary to keep yourself healthy. It will help you select behaviors, from the set of all possible behaviors, which best maintain health. For you, perhaps, it is taking vitamins, washing your hands, keeping dry, whatever your intuition guides you to do. Your unconscious mind will be programmed to take the right actions and your intuition will direct you towards effective choices. You will certainly increase the probability of having fewer colds this winter

You can employ the same process with images in place of words to put intention to work for you. Let a visual representation of your intention arise. Perhaps in the above example it is skiing on a sunny slope in the dead of winter and feeling robust. Recall that image from time to time in your mind's eye. Like an affirmation, it will serve as a subliminal guide to healthy choices and result in increasing the likelihood of your intended outcome.

Finally, earlier we discussed the importance of honoring the truth of your desires even if you do not want them to turn into action. Intention can be used as an antidote to those desires without the harmful intercession of denial.

Excercise

Staying with the example we have been using for this challenge, if you are attracted to someone with whom it would be inappropriate to be intimate, let intention help you. Construct a phrase or visual image which represents the result you want. Perhaps see an image in your mind's eye of you and that person as friends. Or, conversely, repeat from time to time the phrase "I choose to keep a distance from _______ (*fill in the name*)." Without denying what is, this practice can help grow an alternative unconscious program to support you in making the choices you need to keep your life and relationships happy.

Nonattachment

NONATTACHMENT TO OUTCOME is the paradoxical element in the Healing Relationship model. Having hailed the virtue of intention, I am now promoting its apparent opposite: non-attachment. In fact, the two virtues are not in conflict. Intention nests inside non-attachment. Nonattachment is the way in which we hold our intention; loosely and without struggle. We focus on the outcome we desire but we grasp it lightly, with soft hands. We have a clear intention, but we do not clutch at it with the illusion that we have absolute control. We do our best and then accept whatever outcome eventuates.

See it and let it go.
See it and let it go.

See it,
See it,
See it and let it go.

The first six virtues help create the best conditions for healing and relationship building. Then we open our heart and allow the unfolding. We don't try and wrestle reality into the box we have chosen for it. Reality is stronger than we are and the result of a struggle with it has a limited set of outcomes. We either lose, are hurt in the skirmish, or both.

In relationships, non-attachment to outcome is central to real satisfaction. First, nothing kills connection faster than trying to control the other. We create reactivity and rejection. Even if they accept our control, we end up in a dominator-submissive relationship that is death to the vitality of the association.

Nonattachment is also significant because, though commitment is important in relationship, to remain emotionally healthy we can not be dependent upon another for our emotional sustenance. If we try, we paint ourselves into a co-dependent corner in which our well-being is predicated upon someone else's state of mind. This is dysfunctional and ultimately unsatisfactory.

Nonattachment is not a negative state of indifference or lack of caring. It is not a deficiency of interest or commitment. Non-attachment is a positive state of openness and willingness to accept outcome. It implies a faith in the life process that allows relationships and events to develop without coercion. It is acceptance even in the face of aversion. It is accepting dissatisfaction in order to be satisfied.

Nonattachment requires the love, courage, faith, and wisdom to stay with the healing and relationship process until it settles into resolution. If we hold fast to the virtues of the model, the process will likely result in the outcome we desire. When it does not, we need to accept the outcome graciously and move on.

WHEN I WAS LEARNING to lead group process, my teacher, Harry Sloan, emphasized emotional catharsis as the primary modality for emotional healing and growth. He helped people unearth repressed feelings, bring them to awareness, and support them through the process of reliving the discomfort in order to release it. This approach resulted in the visible experience of catharsis and liberation from the hold of old wounds. Harry's work was dramatic to experience and watch. It was impressive to see how fast healing could be facilitated through his methodology around issues that other processes took years or never succeeded in achieving.

I was so impressed and drawn to his style that my initial work mimicked his. Quickly, I became attached to the client always experiencing catharsis. I was determined it should happen. With time and experience, however, I began to realize that my attachment to the client experiencing catharsis was fundamentally coercive.

After studying other styles I learned that dramatic catharsis is not always necessary for healing and growth and that I do not need to be attached to that big release for positive change to occur. I softened my expectations and began to follow the client more than lead them. I became more open to outcome and less attached to catharsis as the mark of a successful transaction.

With that shift, my dropping of attachment to a specific outcome, I became a much better guide. My clients not only did better but felt more free, empowered, and in control of their own growth.

We are all familiar with the experience of someone close being attached to a certain outcome for us. It feels coercive because it is pressure to change from how we are to how they want us to be. It is the opposite of acceptance. Consciously or unconsciously we interpret it as a signal that we are not good enough the way we are.

Someone's effort to control us often sets up the desire to react in the opposite direction. The party attached to the specific outcome feels frustrated and we feel coerced. Attachment to outcome and the resultant control/reaction against control cycle is a major impediment to intimate connection.

The benefits of non-attachment in relationship are many. First, it contributes to the feeling of acceptance, and the experience of being loved unconditionally. One feels honored, respected, and free to be his or herself.

Further, it eliminates the strain that attachment generates for the person trying to control the situation. It is not only an emotional pressure but a physical one also. If you scan your body when you are trying to control someone or are tightly attached to an outcome, you will notice constriction in many places in your body. It is unpleasant and over time can be damaging to health.

ATTACHMENT TO OUTCOME is like carrying an unnecessarily heavy load. There is a story from India illustrating this principle.

A young man decides to take a train journey to the far side of the country. He gathers up his belongings, goes to the station and buys a ticket.

The train is crowded and there is standing room only. After many hours of travel, holding his bags in both hands, he becomes exhausted.

An old man approaches him and asks, "Why are you still holding those suitcases?"

The young traveler replies, "These cases contain things that are very important to me."

The old man answers, "I understand, but you can put them down. The bags will travel with you without the need to carry them the whole way. Let the train do the work."

The story illustrates how the train of life will take us and our hopes and dreams to our intended destination. If we get on the right train and point our self in the right direction, we can release the strain associated with holding fast to our attachments and let Life do the work. We can be free to enjoy the journey.

With an attitude of nonattachment, we are more easily able to open to a flow state within and the truth without. Rather than wrestling reality to fit into our idea, we follow it gracefully and guide it gently. Max Schumpach, a process psychologist, calls this attitude, "respecting nature." It is a respect for the power of the universe as the real controller of events and the knowledge that while we can influence it, we are basically along for the ride.

Humility is the cousin of non-attachment because humility is the knowledge and demonstration that we are not all powerful beings in control of the environment. We can effect events with awareness, truth, acceptance, expression, intuition and intention but we can not determine them.

Nonattachment encourages an experimental attitude. Respecting the awesome nature of the unknown, we point ourselves in the direction we wish to go and then, like the scientist, watch what happens. As data comes in we adjust, giving up what does not work and trying new approaches to test their effectiveness.

IN EASTERN PHILOSOPHICAL traditions, non-attachment is a central theme. One of Buddhism's Four Noble Truth's, the cornerstone of its philosophy, is the truth that attachment leads to suffering. Nonattachment, another of the Four Noble Truths, is "the way out of suffering" and the key to human happiness.

Nonattachment is the central tenet of the Chinese philosophy of Taoism. Tao is defined as the Way, or the natural unobstructed water course. The wise and happy person is the one who goes with the water and does not push the river. The person who suffers is the one who tries to force or control the natural unfolding of events. The same sentiment exists in our Western tradition where scripture invokes us to live such that "Not mine, but divine will be done," and "Not I, but the Father does the work."

The two approaches, East and West, can be integrated within the perspective of the Healing Relationship model. Awareness, Truth, Acceptance, Expression, Intuition, and Intention point us in the direction we want to go.

Respecting non-attachment, we can better honor what is called "resistance" in others. We see it not as a hindrance to our control, but as feedback about what is true for them. Resistance from another to our desired end ought not to be seen as a blocking maneuver but as a healthy reaction and signal to us about where they are and where they want to go. By seeing "resistance" in this way, it is no longer resistance but information. We can drop the burden of struggling to change, conquer, or manipulate the other. We rest in the peace of respecting their view: right, wrong, or indifferent. This also serves to bring mutual regard, which may have slipped into the background, forward in the relationship.

I was meeting with a client organization in San Francisco on a weekly basis to help improve interpersonal relations and further the organization's effectiveness. Before one session, I was told that Ellen, a key employee, was moving out of state and would be leaving the company. I designed an exercise to elicit everyone's appreciations for her and planned to do it at the last session before she left. I thought this would serve both Ellen and the organization. Through it, she would understand the esteem people in the organization held for her and everyone would benefit by experiencing the unique way in which people are appreciated in that company.

When we gathered for the session, I asked the group if we could go forward with this exercise expecting no resistance. I was wrong. Ellen was not up for it at all. "Thanks Howard and everybody," she said, "but I'd rather not. I already know how much you love and appreciate me and that is enough." The usual encouragement failed to sway her.

I was disappointed that my intervention wasn't going to be implemented. I was ready to use the "power of the podium" to force it through. My intuitive voice, however, knew better and told me to honor Ellen's wish. So, I let go.

I asked the group what they wanted to do instead. One man offered the suggestion that we do an exercise we had done some time before using drawing materials. There was general agreement and we went ahead with it. Everyone did a spontaneous drawing and then discussed with the group how they thought it might represent their state of mind.

When it came Ellen's turn to share her drawing, the sadness and grief came pouring out. She spoke of how much she loved working for this company, with these people, and how hard it was to leave. Others responded with how important she was to the organization and to them personally, and how much they were going to miss her. It turned into a love-fest.

This was an important healing experience for Ellen and growth event for the company. Ellen got the support she needed for her transition and the rest of the team bonded at a level deeper than they had before. The outcome was better than anything I could have planned.

By dropping my attachment and allowing an organic synchronicity to guide us, the perfect result, exceeding the result I had hoped for with my predetermined program, was achieved. I was taught the virtue of non-attachment.

✵ ✵ ✵ ✵ ✵

Excercise

To experience the value of non-attachment, try the following exercise. Remember a time recently when someone wanted a certain outcome from you. How did it make you feel? What was your reaction? Was the outcome they wanted forthcoming?

Now, remember a time when you felt wholly uncoerced by another, and you were free to be responsible for yourself. How did that feel and how did you act? What was the outcome?

Recall a time when you yourself were strongly attached to a certain outcome from another. How did it feel?

Recall a time when you really wanted something specific but were able to adjust and open to outcome. How did that feel?

Which of these ways do you prefer to feel? Which way is more effective in the long run for achieving intended outcomes?

✵ ✵ ✵ ✵ ✵

The Processing Relationship

In the context of our most intimate relationship, the couple, it is possible to take the Healing Relationship into its most evolved form, the Processing Relationship. If both people adopt the Healing Relationship attitude, the couple connection itself becomes a path to emotional and spiritual growth.

In the Processing Relationship, whatever arises between the partners is "grist for the mill." Everything, including the unpleasantness, is material for personal and relational growth. The partners "process" the events and feelings of daily life with the goal of healing ourselves and facilitating the growth of the other. This mutual commitment to staying with and working through our personal and interpersonal difficulties is the hallmark of the Processing Relationship.

In the Healing Relationship in general, outside of the context of intimate connection, we do not assume that the other shares our perspective or that they will adopt virtues that parallel our own. We simply live out the seven virtues knowing that it creates an atmosphere in which it is possible for the other to open up to their own healing with no expectation that they will do the same in return. Inevitably, however, it results in deeper more satisfying relationships.

In the Processing Relationship, however, we agree to both adopt the Healing Relationship stance and mutually support the other to heal and grow. When conflict arises between us, we use it to learn about ourselves and set the other free.

Through this process, we both become increasingly spontaneous, less reactive, and more joyful. As we heal through mutual support, we cherish the gift of sharing our lives with another divine Being. We come to see the "problems" in the others character not as flaws but as beauty marks that remind us to cherish them even more.

The greatest challenge in a Processing Relationship is interpersonal conflict. When we are in conflict with our partner, instead of defining him or her as wrong or flawed, we use the circumstances to help ourselves and the other heal and grow. This is an alternative process to fighting with the intention to punish the other for hurting us.

In the Processing Relationship, we combine the techniques of Emotional Release Work discussed in Chapter 4 with the seven elements of the Healing Relationship. That is, we literally facilitate the step by step process in our partners emotional release work, helping guide them into their feelings to gain insight and release from the pain which distresses them. We do so in the context of owning our own feelings, sharing them truthfully, and constructing our action from a base of intuition, intention, and non-attachment.

This is imperfectly summarized in a small piece called "The Courage to Love," whose author is unknown. I have taken the liberty to reconstruct it into the form of vows we can offer each other, committing ourselves to a Processing Relationship.

- I'm willing to use whatever arises in this relationship for my own awakening and the awakening of my partner.
- When we are in conflict, I will always ask myself the following questions:
- What am I experiencing right now in body sensations and emotions?

- What emotional charge do I bring to this situation and how am I participating in creating this situation?
- What truth do I need to tell? What is the most vulnerable truth I can tell, with no blame or judgment?
- What can I do right now that will support my intention to use whatever arises for awakening?

CHAPTER ELEVEN

Communication, Conflict, & Cooperation

When truth is buried underground it grows, it chokes,
it gathers such an explosive force that on the day it bursts out,
it blows up everything with it.
Emile Zola

OMMUNICATION IS THE FOUNDATION upon which relationships are built. It is the master tool that creates long lasting bonds. Communication prevents the build up of the corrosive material that destroys relationships and is the skill needed to handle conflict. If there is any such thing as a magic bullet that turns conflict into co-operation, it is communication. When relationships become damaged, communication is the means for repair. Communication serves as both prevention and treatment in almost all areas of human relations.

Our society does not sufficiently honor the value of communication. In fact, it often diminishes its importance. Especially for men, the ethic of machismo emphasizes speaking little, sharing less, and not revealing our feelings. The less we say the more macho we appear. The less we communicate, the better we manufacture an image of strength. The consequences of these values are poor communication skills and large amounts of unresolved resentment and interpersonal conflict.

Our underdeveloped standards around communications are represented and modeled to us by the values defining institutions of our social structure. The communication style used in government, economic, and cultural institutions, for instance, are regularly shared with us through the media. As models for effective communication they are a disaster. Public discourse is carried on at very low levels of sophistication. So low, our institutional leaders sometimes appear like five-year-olds tweaking their noses and calling each other names.

The diplomatic discourse around the recent famine in North Korea is a good example. The famine was becoming increasingly serious and hundreds of thousands of people were in danger of death by starvation. The U.S. State Department said to the North Koreans, "We will give you money to buy food if you agree to talks with South Korea on normalizing relations." In response, the North Koreans said, "We will talk with South Korea, but only after you give us money."

The State Department replied like any self respecting five-year-old, "Nuh, uh. You show me yours first." In response, the North Koreans rose to the occasion with "Nuh, uh. You first, too."

Another aspect of our value system that inhibits effective communication is our "rugged individualism"—the belief that we should take care of our problems alone. That we are stronger better people if we work disagreements out without involving others. Though this approach has theoretical merit, in reality few of us are sufficiently evolved spiritually or psychologically to make it work. Indeed, our individualism fosters an avoidance of necessary communication. There is no way around open communication if we want healthy satisfying human connection.

Communication

EFFECTIVE COMMUNICATION is not about mastering skills or techniques, neither is it about learning fancy phrases or stringing together the right words in the right order. Effective communication is fundamentally about integrity, attitude, and intention. If we speak our truth directly, clearly, and honestly with an attitude of love, then our communication will be effective. We can study all the books on communication, take all the courses, learn exactly which pronoun goes where, but without integrity, or the proper attitude and intention, our communication will fail.

Communication involves a sending component and a receiving component. Receiving or listening is the more important element in effective communication. Listening is paying close attention to what is said while at the same time making an unqualified effort to understand the meaning fully.

Good listening simply requires the commitment to receiving the other just as they are, without any effort to change them. It requires an attitude of learner rather than teacher. When we understand that we can learn from the unique perspective of every person we listen to, then listening becomes a rewarding enterprise.

The major blocks to listening are egoism and impatience. We think we can't learn from the other so we don't pay attention. Or, we give some future task or person higher priority, and in our haste we do not give ourselves fully to listening to the person before us.

To be a good listener is to be a good human being. We must be sufficiently developed to understand that others are worthy of our love; to know that everyone is uniquely interesting and valuable, and that they qualify for our full attention when they speak.

The mechanics of listening, as taught by the communication company Highgain, can be summarized with the acronym, AAA: *Allow, Accept, Acknowledge.*

Allow the other person to have her view, without trying to change it.

Accept what she says as valuable, whether or not we agree with it, because the person speaking is intrinsically valuable.

Acknowledge what has been communicated by indicating that you have heard, received, and understood the message, even though this does not necessarily mean agreement.

The second dimension in the communication equation—sending information or speaking—depends upon the integrity of the speaker. Making one's self understood in a direct, clear, truthful manner, without any effort to manipulate is the hallmark of effective speech.

The four elements that constitute effective speech are: frequency, openness, directness, and honesty. Conversely, infrequency, closedness, indirection, and manipulation characterize poor communication.

THE FIRST ELEMENT is frequency. Frequency is important because to remain current with people, to be present with them, it is necessary to share our experience with them consistently and over time. In intimate relationships it is critical to communicate even the small details of our lives. Often, it is the omission of the details of our experience that makes people feel distant from us. Sharing that we are touched by Mark McGwire's breaking Babe Ruth's home run record or that we are disturbed by the garbage collector having missed collection day lets people in on who we are and how we are presently.

This is especially true for disturbances that arise between people, even the seemingly mundane. The apparently insignificant items like, "I wish you wouldn't put that hot cup of coffee on the new table" or "It didn't feel good when you told Bill that I don't like his sister." These are the kinds of feelings we talk ourselves out of sharing because they appear trivial and may cause conflict. However, these little matters constitute the fabric of our lives. In the long run, sharing them actually builds bonds, even if they make waves in the short run. Withholding our feelings of agitation, even about small matters, eventually builds into resentment and will sabotage the quality of our relationships.

THE SECOND ELEMENT is openness. As a rule, unless there is a compelling reason not to, if the urge arises to share some piece of our experience, it is worth sharing. Open communication means minimizing self-censorship and secrecy. Self-censoring is the tendency to reject the act of sharing after the awareness or urge to communicate has arisen. Censoring is rooted in an effort to give out only the information we feel is sufficiently sanitized to maintain a narrowly defined public image of ourselves, rather than sharing the full complexity of who we are. In the end, it erodes the basis for intimacy and sets the table for long-term discord.

Others do not know what is going on in the little black box of our personality unless we tell them. To generate understanding we need to share our thoughts and feelings. We force others into incorrect assumptions based on insufficient evidence if we only dribble out what we think is safe for their consumption.

Secrecy is a killer. Not the secrecy of keeping another's confidence, but the hiding of one's own experience. It hurts the person keeping the secret as well as the people from whom the secret is kept. Secrets are like a drop of ink in a pool of clear water. Just a little bit pollutes an otherwise clean system. Because few secrets ever remain hidden, they often alienate the person with whom we do not share. Inevitably they come out into the open in some unhealthy manner and those who learn that they have not been trusted with our confidence feel belittled and estranged.

Without open communication, people's sense of who you are is more about their psychological process than yours. The less you share of your experience and who you are, the more you become a blank screen for others to project their own experience upon. This can make your life very confusing and is the source of much interpersonal conflict. Openly communicating our experience helps create a more unified and mutually agreed upon definition of who we are and a basis for more cooperative relationships.

THE THIRD ELEMENT in effective communication, directness, can be simply defined by the old adage, "Say what you mean and mean what you say." Don't beat around the bush for the purpose of impression management. Don't get diverted from the truth of your communication by focusing all of your energy on being diplomatic, trying to use the right words to avoid a negative response. All that "trying" and effort to control the situation is generated by fear. Just "say what you mean and mean what you say," holding love in your heart while you do so.

When love is the field within which you communicate, it is possible to be direct without putting the other on the defensive. The positive regard with which the message is delivered allows it to be received with that intent.

Get in touch with your heartfelt truth and let the words flow, the right words will emerge in the right order, naturally, without trying. Don't think too much, don't lose your truth in the rehearsing. Speak your truth directly, with love.

The most challenging time to be direct, of course, is when we think the other person is not going to like our message. In these circumstances, we may try to soften the message by padding it with nice. Too easily, nice becomes a muddled, insincere, confused message.

Sometimes, when we are concerned about the someone's reaction, we avoid communicating at all. This is the worst alternative. It confuses every one. It is far better for relationships to speak the difficult truth directly and without guile than to suffer the long-term consequences of avoidance and denial. Spoken directly, with love in the heart, even difficult information will likely be received and understood.

In effective communication, it is not the construction of the words or sentence pattern that is central to the process. It is the attitude we hold toward the other when we speak. Having said that, I would like to share a helpful guideline for communicating our thoughts and feelings that was taught to me by Angeles Arien.

The guideline consists of four elements we share with the person to whom we are speaking. They are:

I see . . . .
I feel . . . .
I want . . . .
I'm willing . . . .

"I see" involves telling the other what it is about their behavior I am having a reaction to. The second element, "I feel," states our emotional reaction to that behavior. "I want" makes a positive statement about how I would like it to be. And finally, "I'm willing" offers what I am prepared to do to contribute to a mutually beneficial end.

So, for example, if my brother Jerry isn't helping me to care for my aged mother and I'm angry about that, but I don't know what to say or do, I can use this formula to help me construct a response.

"Look Jerry, *I see* that I'm the one who provides almost all the care for Mother. *I feel* angry and resentful that I have to spend so much time away from my own wife and kids to do it. *I want* you to help me more and share this burden more equally with me. *I'm willing* to do my part if you do yours."

To help the subsequent conversation be more constructive, you can use the same elements as prompts. Ask each as a question, one at a time, and listen attentively to their answer before prompting with the next element. "What do you see?." "How do you feel ?" "What do you want?" and "What are you willing to do?"

Of course, people are not robots and will not necessarily fall in to lock step answering in an orderly fashion. However, asking the questions when it is appropriate can be a great help in facilitating direct and open communication during difficult circumstances.

Indirect communication is usually the result of surrendering to fear. We are afraid of the other's response, so we swallow our thoughts and feelings without sharing them. Both approaches, evasion and avoidance, have the long-term consequence of diminishing the quality of connectedness in the relationship.

I recently observed an example of evasion and avoidance and its resultant negative effect on a previously happy relationship. The training director of a steel plant put a television in the employee break room so that later in the day he could show training videos to the new hires. One of the workers, a friend and former workmate of the training director, didn't like having the electrical cord running across the area where he sat during his lunch. Without saying anything to the safety director he moved the TV to a location where it was out of his way. When the training director returned to the break room and saw the television moved to a different place without his knowledge, he got angry. Without knowing or asking who had done it, he cursed for all to hear, "Mother fucker, stupid asshole."

When the worker who moved the television in the first place heard through the grapevine about this comment, he assumed the words were meant personally for him. Because both men evaded and avoided communicating directly about the problem during and after its occurrence, the feelings on both sides went sour. The friendship was ruined. If they had addressed it directly, a friendship could have been saved. By having gone through the difficulty together, it may have even deepened.

Similarly, in a parts shop in Detroit, I noticed that one of the machinists, Jake, was becoming alienated from his fellow workers. I asked him what was going on. "I have no idea," he told me. "The only thing I know for sure is that I am being iced out."

I inquired with the other machinists and discovered that they had a good deal of resentment towards Jake. They told me that they were angry with him because he arrived late to work almost everyday and they felt they had to pick up his slack without extra compensation. "While we bust our ass to get to work on time, he strolls in at 9 or 10 o'clock and never says a word about it."

When I spoke with Jake again and told him why people were angry he was dumbfounded. "That makes no sense. Before I hired on I made an agreement with the boss to have flexible work hours. I'm a single dad with no reliable child care and it often causes me to be late. But I always make up my hours and my work at the end of the day or on the weekends." I checked with the owner and he confirmed that this was true.

No one told the other shop employees about this arrangement. They assumed Jake was a slacker and they were having to pull an extra load to carry him. Steeped in the same values and fears we have been discussing, they didn't confront him or talk to anyone else directly about their concerns. They preferred to gossip about Jake and "ice him out."

When I became aware of the confused picture, I encouraged Jake and the others to talk about it directly, but they refused. They made up excuses. Everyone let the situation drag on, hoping it would go away, but it got worse. This is the normal course of the denial and avoidance process. The resentment built to massive levels and when it became intolerable Jake quit.

This could have been a simple problem to fix. All it would have taken was clear direct communication and the likelihood that it would have resolved favorably was high. Jake would have had the job he wanted, his work mates would have understood the morning start time issue, and the shop would have had a stronger more able team. Instead an unhappy shop lost a valuable employee and virtually nothing was learned to help avoid a similar calamity from happening again.

THE FOURTH ELEMENT in effective communication is honesty. Truth between people is fundamental to building and maintaining trust. Honesty is what creates trust, and trust is a cornerstone of good relationships. Where there is trust we can endure the challenges which all relationships face. We can "hang in" for the ups and downs of disagreement and conflict when there is fundamental trust between people.

I awoke from a dream the other day with these words resonating in my mind, "It is better to speak the truth of our pain, than to spout sweet platitudes about peace." We may say nice things, eloquent things, smart things, but what especially connects us in life is sharing how it really is for us.

I was sitting on the beach with my friend David. The discussion turned to the parade of beautiful women who were walking the beach in scant bikinis. We mused about how our wives would react observing us watching this tantalizing show. Could we be honest about the attraction we felt toward these women or would we have to fake it, pretending we were unmoved for the sake of impression management.

David said that forgetting about the "right and wrong" of it, as a practical matter, the truth however disturbing, usually leads to a more satisfactory outcome than misrepresentation. He said, "Telling the truth, even when we think the other person is not going to like it, is a pay as you go plan. You're always caught up and you are always even and there are no heavy dues to pay later. Pay now and it's over with."

If we are honest even with the difficult truths, we can deal with the consequence while they are still small and manageable. If we withhold the truth it will eventually leak out, and when it does, there is a big bill with interest due.

One of the excuses we give ourselves for avoiding speaking honestly is that we are afraid we may hurt another's feelings. Of course; underneath that worry is the more significant fear that if we hurt the other they will hurt us in return. It is easier to be honest when we understand that most of the time, even if the other is hurt and reacts negatively, the overall pain for both parties is minimized by "paying now instead of later." This is stated beautifully in a line from a popular song, "I'd rather hurt you honestly than mislead you with a lie."

The courage that honesty demands is the courage to be one's true self publicly; to share who we are, as we are, what we are truly thinking and feeling whether others like it or not. To whom do we owe the most allegiance, ourselves or others? Is it worth propping up an image of ourselves to others at the cost of self-deception? Can we really afford this lie? To be in support of our self, we must have the courage to speak our truth and let others have their own feelings without trying to manage their response.

This, of course, is easier said than done. Honesty is both a high and challenging standard, but it is practical, functional, and healthy. Honesty allows us to maintain one of our most prized possessions: self respect. In the long run, whatever minor hits we may take as a result of being in defense of our integrity, it builds and maintains relationships in a way that few other qualities will.

Honest communication is the challenge of integrating head and heart; to unite our thoughts with our feelings and communicate them authentically. In this unity, we don't operate, as is our habit, with our heads alone, calculating what will maximize our image in the moment. We don't act from emotion alone, spraying out whatever feelings arise in the moment without regard for others. We combine cognition and emotion, telling the truth with love. The difficulty of this challenge was stated by Pope John XXIII when he said, "The longest journey is from the head to the heart."

Poor communication is marked by characteristics opposite of those described above. Poor communication is infrequent, indirect, unrevealing, and manipulative. It is infrequent in that a person rarely speaks, and when he does, he shares minimally, communicating the least information necessary to get by. This is the attitude of "cool." Unfortunately, in our country, it is part of the macho ethic and as such is a highly valued standard, particularly in the mainstream masculine culture. It truly turns out to be "cool" in that it results in a lack of warmth in one's life.

Ineffective communication is unrevealing in that little is disclosed about the true nature of one's inner process. This is summed up in the Henry Ford III quote of Disraeli, "Never complain, never explain. " It sounds savvy, it would make good patter in a movie, but it is hell on relationships. It may be functional in some extreme situations not to share the turmoil inside, but in normal life it is creates an iron barrier between people. When we don't share what we are experiencing with others, we place them on shaky grounds.

They don't know the context they are operating in, or whether it is safe interpersonal territory. When trust is not present the normal reaction is to keep one's distance.

Ineffective communication is indirect in that it does not go straight to the point. In fact, it is designed to avoid the point while giving the impression that something of substance is being said. The speaker may eventually get around to it but the concealment used to soften the message makes it hard to find amongst the camouflage. The listener becomes confused and irritated. When she finally gets through the bramble and understands, she may already be bored, angry or indifferent.

Indirect communication is also manipulative, the fourth characteristic of poor communication. Manipulation is about control, and is not focused on sending a clear message but rather on controlling communication so as to control people and events. Because our perspectives are so narrow and our understanding of the moment so constrained, manipulative communication seldom results in the desired outcome, even when the manipulation is successful. It does result, however, in causing resentment in the person being manipulated and the diminishment of the quality of that relationship.

Even the most skillful manipulation generally ends up being transparent. With the clarity of hindsight, sooner or later, the manipulation is seen for it's duplicity. The next interaction will be marked by hostility, defensiveness, or at the least reserve. Whatever the specific outcome of manipulation, its overall effect is the diminishment of connection.

Poor communication drives away relationships, alienates others, and isolates one's self. Unfortunately, examples of poor communication abound. They arise numerous times every day in the course of our normal lives. They are far more common than examples of effective communication.

To communicate well and effectively it is important to avoid power struggles. They seldom result in satisfaction for either party. We may win and overpower the other, but winning is not necessarily a happy ending.

I find the most useful stance to hold in communication with others is that of the perennial learner, gaining new knowledge, through the library of other people's wisdom. If we listen non-judgmentally and state our opinions without coercion, others are willing to share their well thought out (or not so well thought out) perspectives with us. Later, in privacy and quiet, we can synthesize and integrate this new knowledge, accepting what is useful and discarding what is not.

I often see couples in intimate relationships stuck in unconscious patterns of chronic power struggle. It becomes a habit with which they make themselves miserable. I was working with a couple like this recently. They were captured by their own constantly repeating cycle of struggles for dominance. Neither was able to hear or respond to the other's pain because they were not listening. While one spoke the other was focused on how to leverage what they said for their next move in getting the upper hand. The strategy never worked for either of them. They constantly struggled with each other, emotionally bloodying themselves to a painful and pathetic pulp. Neither changed their strategy nor stopped trying to impose their will on the other, despite the obvious feedback that what they were doing was not working. They were more interested in being right then being happy.

It is important to recognize when we are in a habitual power struggle and remember to pull the cord, hop off that bus, and get on a different one that has a better chance of taking us where we want to go. Verbally going around in circles over similar territory and not getting anywhere is what I call cycling. Cycling is the primary indicator that we are not at the core of the difference, but stuck in a power struggle.

Recognizing when we are stuck in such a cycle is the first step toward breaking it. If we can let go of the need to be right and for the other to accept our view, we can shift from the teacher role, giving information and demanding compliance, to the more useful learner role, and relax into listening and receiving.

Once the other person feels that you have shifted out of the power struggle, and they sense they are truly being listened to, the drive to impose their views on you is drained. They know they have been received and feel accepted, even if they know you do not agree with them. That gives them the freedom to let go of trying to jam it down your throat. The possibility is created for mutual understanding, respect, and harmony even without agreement.

To avoid power struggles, it helps if we shift our habit when communicating with others from looking for where they are wrong to looking for where they are right. We are conditioned since childhood to hold a critical perspective; to look for where the other is mistaken in order to gain an advantage. We are taught this critical perspective at home and in school. Later, it becomes a habit and we become addicted to the negative energy bundled into it in the same way people become addicted to gossip.

But looking for defects in others or their opinions does not serve us. It produces division and acrimony. It does not yield balance. There are alternative and superior strategies. Try looking for what is right in the other and their opinions. Come together through that, and later, where there are differences, a valuable exchange is possible.

This small shift in perspective can result in a sea change in relationships. Others will feel heard, accepted, and comfortable. We ourselves will be more warmly received. It is a shift from disconnection to connection and it works.

Conflict

COMMUNICATION NOT ONLY nurtures relationship, it is also the primary tool with which we can transform conflict into personal growth and interpersonal cooperation. Conflict begins with difference. Difference in desires, interests, and perspectives. Difference escalates into hostility when we perceive it as a threat to our getting what we want. Then, difference becomes antagonism and conflict arises. The hostility creates yet more antipathy and interpersonal distance. Distance reduces the likelihood of cessation of conflict because the central resolving mechanism—communication—is not in play.

Where communication is diminished, misunderstanding and distrust grows, fueling the flames of conflict. The pattern is obvious and easy to see when one is outside of it, but when we are involved in it, we are often blinded by the anger and hurt that accompanies conflict. Feelings can heat up to such an extent that the parties feel it's impossible even to allow themselves to talk with the other, let alone try to understand their differences.

The tendency to slip into conflict, and once having fallen into it of being unable to get out of it, is the reason constant interpersonal processing to clear up minor differences is so important. It is critically important in our most intimate relationships: with spouses, children, and work mates. Dialog needs to be ongoing with all the relevant issues aired, misunderstandings cleared, and understanding generated. Understanding, not agreement, is the key factor. It is not critical that people agree for them to be in harmony. But it is critical that they understand each other. Understanding allows differences to exist without hostility or division. With understanding, differences remain manageable rather than escalating into harmful conflict. It may even become a source of interest and spice.

This is why at the international level the diplomatic strategy of engagement is almost always more effective than disengagement when the goal is peace making. Engagement without appeasement, even with the enemy, is more effective than exclusion and separation. With engagement, communication remains possible. Consequently, the best tool for resolving conflict is in place and at the proper moment it is available to help reduce hostility and foster peace.

I was reminded of how ineffectual power struggles in human relations are by a dream I had. The main character in the dream, Joel, an actual person from a client organization, is a very political, argumentative man. In the dream Joel is saying something I don't agree with. I feel an immediate urge and a sense of obligation to state my contrary opinion, and I do. He finds fuel in some of my words and continues arguing, jacking up the energy a few more notches. It became very much like the scenario I described with the husband and wife in their chronic destructive power struggles.

In the dream, though, I remembered that there is a choice point in these interactions. I could continue to struggle, pushing my argument against the stone wall of Joel's opposition and exhaust myself. Or, I could release the inner tension and attachment to changing his opinion and relax into listening. As a beneficial side effect I really listened to Joel's message and understood it. Even without agreement, the heat cooled down to a comfortable ember.

I felt, in the dream, at a physical-body level, the habitual urge to engage in struggle; to fight and overpower the other with my ideas so that he would change his mind and agree with me. Instead, I chose the wiser course and stopped trying to convince him of anything. Immediately, I noticed a delicious, almost ecstatic, sense of relief and freedom.

It is that choice point, where we unconsciously fall into interpersonal power struggles, that we need to learn to make conscious and identify so we can deal with conflict more skillfully. We can learn to identify the internal cues that push us unwittingly forward when we begin to gear up for battle. By studying ourselves and learning what our own internal cues are—particularly body signs like constriction in the throat or tightening of the hands—we can enter into conflict consciously, or gracefully avoid it. If we choose the strategy of battle, we can go into it with awareness, knowing the difficulties that will inevitably arise, so that when they do we will not be deterred from our goal. Simply put, we need to learn not to get sucked into conflict, but to choose it or choose to avoid it.

Power struggling is a habit not confined to those unsophisticated in matters psychological and spiritual. I saw a New Age icon on the television show "Politically Correct" in a conversation with three other guests. This intelligent and articulate proponent of New Age beliefs, fell into a power struggle with the unconscious ease of an adolescent. He was making an insightful and useful point about how the others guests' anger at President Clinton's sexual escapades were arising more out of their projections than Clinton's behavior. He cited as evidence the inappropriately venomous nature of their criticism.

Though he was clearly correct in his analysis, because the others didn't agree with him, he wouldn't let go. He hit their bait of rejection like a fish after a shiny lure. Because they didn't reply to his insightful observation with agreement, he continued at them mercilessly. Everyone, the host, the other guests, and the audience tuned him out and went on with their own agenda. He gave the impression of a spurned child whining in the background. Falling unconsciously into power struggles is not only exhausting, frustrating and fruitless, it makes us look silly.

Because we are so habituated to power struggling, some people unthinkingly assume difference is opposition. Others see opposition everywhere, it becomes their working assumption. Often, we don't listen closely enough to know whether someone's views and interests are compatible or incompatible with our own. The assumption of opposition can elicit immediate offensive or evasive action.

I call this syndrome The Myth of Opposition. It is prevalent in people who come from families steeped in conflict, accusation, and blame. They are more comfortable with conflict because it is the atmosphere they are accustomed to and may actually be uncomfortable with harmony because it is so unfamiliar.

The Myth of Opposition is also learned as a child in school or as an adult working in dysfunctional organizations. The Myth of Opposition is widespread in the workplace. It is a common reason why it is sometimes so hard to get simple things done in organizations: before starting a project or task there already exists a wall of opposition, whatever the merits or demerits of the program.

Sometimes in the work setting I begin to say something to someone and he reflexively assumes a defensive posture. His immediate assumption is that what I am going to say is going to be a problem for him. I find this response frustrating and upsetting because my intention is to help. Still, I have learned that from a practical point of view the only strategy that allows me to keep my dignity and calm is not to slide unconsciously into struggle. Instead, I try to notice my internal cues and use them as a warning alarm to avoid getting sucked into conflict. I speak what I have to say and leave it at that.

Through this behavior, I break their belief that interaction necessarily results in struggle and conflict. It reduces the strength of their combative reaction. As the relationship matures, interaction becomes more pleasant and productive.

Blame is a communication killer and the enemy of good relationships. If skillful communication is the glue of a relationship, then blame is the solvent that dissolves it.

It is a important to avoid blame in all communication and interpersonal affairs. If there is a problem, the best approach is problem solving, not blaming. Separating the deed from the doer makes this easier. The error is condemnable, not the person.

Cooperation: The Way Out is Through

ONCE CONFLICT HAS BEGUN, communication provides the path back to cooperation. Though it is possible for an individual to release animosity and forgive unilaterally, conflict resolution without the participation of both parties is rare. On the other hand, resolving conflict through communication is almost always possible. To be effective, communication must meet the previously stated standards of frequency, openness, directness, and honesty.

The way out of conflict is through communication and into cooperation. This is called "processing." We talk about, or process, our differences until resolution is reached. We stay connected with each other, even if there is anger, sadness, or hurt. We stay engaged even when we aren't liking the other; even when it's really uncomfortable.

When we want to run away and hide, we don't—we stay until there is understanding. We process until we understand the source and it either dissolves or we allow the conflict to stand without any need to change it.

Continuous processing in intimate relationships and the work place is the best way to maintain healthy, happy, productive connections. Continuous processing means addressing the hundreds of small differences that arise in the normal course of a relationship. It is like food preparation. When we prepare food to nourish our body, waste is naturally generated. Dishes, pots, and pans get dirty and garbage is created. Similarly, in the normal course of human interaction garbage is produced. It needs to be cleaned up continuously just like the kitchen.

Unfortunately, we have come to believe that the constantly arising but mundane interpersonal glitches that we experience in the course of relationships are too petty to address. We tell ourselves we shouldn't be bothered. We should get over it on our own. But we are bothered and we don't get over it.

Every time we swallow one of those interpersonal discomforts instead of discussing it, a seed of resentment is planted. The more of these "petty" differences that we do not process, the more the seed grows until it turns into a whole garden of resentment. While it is growing, distance is building between people. Inevitably, the resentment explodes into open hostility. This volcanic reaction is destructive because it is generated by past events that have gone unprocessed. It is out of proportion to the present circumstances and thus feels frightening and crazy.

If differences are addressed when they are small, giant gulfs do not build up nor do destructive outbursts tend to arise. Our processing removes the garbage while it is of manageable proportions.

THERE IS A CONTINUUM of depth ranging from the superficial to the profound that describes various approaches to conflict resolution. Strategies that focus on the actual content of the struggle are aimed at facilitating mutual understanding without necessarily achieving agreement or healing. This level of intervention is sufficient for many conflicts and allows the discussion and relationship to keep moving forward so that when the time is ripe agreement or a more profound understanding may be reached.

Agreeing to disagree is achieved through the all-important act of attentively listening, and, to the extent possible, putting ourselves in the shoes of the other. The understanding and empathy that naturally flows from vigilant listening diminishes the tendency to judge and categorize, making room for cooperation in the presence of difference. It softens the edges around the right/wrong classification habit we easily fall into. If we agree to disagree, we avoid the conflict producing trap of "I am right and you are wrong." Instead we have a paradigm where the issue is not "I'm good, you're bad," but "we are different, and that's okay."

A more in depth approach to conflict resolution is presented by Roger Fischer and William Ury in their book *Getting to Yes*. Fischer and Ury developed their ideas through many years of empirical study. They emphasize going beneath the participants' "positions," the actual content that is generating the conflict, to discover the "interests" that are generating each position. At the level of interests there is infinitely more flexibility and ground for mutual agreement.

Once the underlying interests are identified, participants need to look for the ways in which the interests are compatible. This results in generating solutions that serve both parties interests and result in win-win solutions. When the argument remains stuck in the narrowly defined terms of positions, participants feel driven into the fighting mode. For me to win, you must lose, and vice-versa.

For example, on the surface, I have a conflict with my wife about buying a sofa for the living room. She wants one; I don't. She can argue until the moon turns blue about the advantages of having a sofa. I can argue endlessly about the disadvantages. Neither of us will convince the other if we maintain the conflict at this level of positions.

Of course, one of us could capitulate, negate our own position and let the other have his or her way. This doesn't really work because it avoids the problem for present but plants the seed of resentment for the future. That seed will grow with other negated interests and will arise at some future time, sparked by some other minor difference, and generate an even more heated conflict than the present one.

The "getting to yes" methodology asks each of us to explore our interests which lie below the position that we are adamantly pursuing. My interest, below my opposition to the sofa, is that I like open space. I don't want more things in the living room cluttering it up. If we get a sofa, I'm afraid we will lose the open airy feeling we have now.

The interest behind Barbara's position to buy a sofa is that she wants a place to be able to get really comfortable in the living room. She wants a piece of furniture where she can rest and relax. That is something we presently don't have.

At this level of discussion, it is immediately clear that there is mutuality of interests. Barbara likes the open uncluttered feeling as I do and I would like to be able to relax more comfortably in the living room as she does. Starting from that place of mutuality of interests, it was easy to arrive at a solution through cooperative problem solving. We decided to buy a smaller sofa, something just a bit bigger than a love set but smaller than the idea I had in my head of what Barbara wanted. Further, we figured out a way to place it in the room so that its visual impact was minimized. Also, we decided to take down some things from the walls to make the room look and feel more spacious.

By going beneath the surface positions to the true interests, a solution was easily discovered. It not only resolved the conflict but created a solution that was better for both of us than either of the original positions would have been had there been a winner and loser.

When conflict becomes chronic, then we know the source of conflict resides not in the precipitating issues but elsewhere. When this is the case, it is necessary to move farther along the conflict resolution continuum toward the deeper levels of intervention and identify what needs to be released or healed.

Cycling of conflict, the repetition of the same antagonism in different guises, indicates that the conflict resolution strategy needs to go deeper to the source if it is to be resolved. Chronic conflict is seldom about one person being right and the other wrong. It is about emotional wounding and how that hurt is being reactivated in the present.

The most profound and effective solution to chronic conflict lies in emotional release work. It is our emotional response to disagreement that generates conflict, not the difference itself. By beginning with the feelings that are arising within us during conflict, and using them as the basis for emotional release work, we can find our way out of many chronic and disturbing conflicts. We drop deeply into the feelings and stay with them until insight as to their origin arises and/or the blocked energy dissipates.

Images may arise and we can dialog with them, or a place in our body may reveal the hidden source that is driving our feelings and our side of the conflict. Whatever technique we use for the emotional release process, we focus on ourselves as the source of the blockage and work to heal it. When we do the inner work it shifts the nature of the external conflict. Either it loosens its driving energy and disappears or its intensity is substantially reduced.

Whatever the nature of the specific conflict, it calls forth previously hidden wounded areas within ourselves that are now ready to be healed. In this way, if we take responsibility for our feelings, conflict can be a gift.

If all the partners in a relationship are awake to this truth, they can help each other grow. If each facilitates the other's emotional release work, then there will be true continuous processing. When people do this for each other, the surface conflict is solved with ease and the personal growth is profound. The conflict is unlikely to rise again because it is addressed and resolved at the causal level. The seed is gone, it will no longer grow, nor will it produce the fruit of conflict.

Additionally, when people engage in this work together, intimacy is generated. Understanding and compassion expand; defensiveness is diminished because they learn they are with, not against, each other.

RECENTLY, I WAS WORKING with two partners who own a successful retail store. They are good friends but have chronic conflicts. When they are in conflict, anything one says the other finds fault with and reacts against it. When they get stuck like this they call me to help loosen the bind.

Together we engage in a process similar to that described above, and invariably we get down to real solutions that work. In this way, little by little, we chip away and remove the sources of conflict. The job, however, is not yet complete.

The last time I worked with them they were locked in a battle over how to compensate their sales staff; how to pay and motivate them to higher levels of performance. They were conflict cycling, talking in circles, dropping complex numbers and abstract concepts on each other, but making no progress toward resolution.

I began facilitating the process of John, who was having the strongest emotional reaction. The very strength of his response was an indicator of his readiness to release the source of the feelings. I slowed him down and led him into the body responses associated with his feelings. Slowly, with a bit of quiet time passing, he began to see relationships between the present, the feelings being generated within him, and their roots in his history.

The aggressive posture John held toward his partner was connected to his lifelong attempts to impress his father. As a child he did it by asserting his scholastic and mathematical acumen. Now, he was reenacting the response with his partner, John's senior in age and experience, and somewhat of a father figure to him. He used a similar process: desperately trying to be right about the numbers. When he understood this in himself, the situation shifted from intensely serious to lighthearted and almost humorous. He let go of his stranglehold on the need to be right and was able for the first time to really listen to his partner. Once he truly listened, his part-

CHAPTER TWELVE

Time, Family, & Work Life

We are poisoned by the hypnotic belief that good things come only from unceasing striving and tireless effort. "I am busy," we say this with no small degree of pride, as if our exhaustion were a trophy, and our ability to withstand stress a badge of true Spiritual character.
Wayne Muller

Time

S TRESS IS EPIDEMIC. The pace of our society is so hurried and the expectations so high, that many of us are living in a chronic state of discord and imbalance. Those who have achieved the pinnacle of our material culture are living on the edge of burn out and exhaustion.

For some, it feels impossible to escape the ceaseless demands of time. The new work ethic is: Do more to fall less far behind. In some professional settings, twelve hour days are the norm. Even less demanding occupations increasingly call for more and more time "at the office."

The state of our technology allows it to follow us most anywhere at any time of day. It catches us at home, in the car, even in the woods or at the beach. Our cell phones, faxes, laptop computers are ever ready to put us in touch with more busy-ness. They all spell *d-e-m-a-n-d*. These hi-tech wonders that make us more productive, also call us away from the activities that can restore our inner harmony and external balance: solitude, quiet, and reflection.

LONG HOURS AND A fast pace leave us confused and dissatisfied, wondering, "How can I shift things around to devote more time to myself, family, friends, and community." This orientation is what I call, "How do I move the furniture around in my life?" What do I subtract, what do I add, what kind of redistribution and rearrangements do I need to make in order to create a more satisfying lifestyle. This approach is seldom effective. It is fundamentally a mechanical approach to an organic problem. The method does not fit the nature of the dilemma, so it doesn't have a successful outcome.

The strategy of trying to redistribute time to the various external segments of our lives does not challenge the actual causal factors that have created the imbalance in the first place. It does not address the underlying assumptions at the root of the dilemma. It is working at the level of effect rather than cause. It is moving furniture to solve the problem of the floor caving in.

Rearranging schedules, adding, subtracting, and dividing time does not touch the fundamental cause of the imbalance: loss of direct contact with our inner well of harmony, our Essence. If we cultivate the inner life, balance will emerge in our external lives without so much heavy lifting.

The only real solution to this so called "lack of time" is profoundly knowing that our foremost priority is nurturing the Self; remembering who we are, cultivating our Spiritual life, and feeling our feelings. Then, behaviors which naturally result in creating an appropriate balance between work and family life will follow and our time will be allocated appropriately.

The belief that we do not have enough time and that work and family are two conflicting options is based on false assumptions. There is not really a lack of time, rather a confusion about the priorities which guide the allocation of the time we have. Whatever the claims of the modern work place, including its technological extensions, the demands alone do not make decisions for us. Nor do the demands themselves allocate our time. We choose among them based on our conscious or unconscious priorities.

We make choices based upon what is most important to us. The solution to creating balance from imbalance is to bring our priorities into consciousness and let them guide our behavior.

The aphorism, "No one ever wrote on their tombstone, I wish I had spent more time at the office," is both funny and true. Death is perhaps our greatest teacher. When we become conscious of its inevitability, through the passing of someone dear to us, our priorities quickly become clear. What is important and what is trivial emerges from the shroud of unconsciousness that we hide behind, living in denial and avoidance of death.

What is more important to us: career, money, power, recognition, and fame? Or, awakening to the love in our hearts and sharing it with others? Cherishing the people close to us or butting heads in competition so we can die with more toys than the next guy? If you knew you were going to die tomorrow, what would you do today?

❈ ❈ ❈ ❈ ❈

Excercise

Spiritual teacher and writer Stephen Levine took a year to explore this question. He devoted an entire year to living as if it were his last. He, as would we, became very clear about what is important and what is not. Time disappeared as a problem.

What would you learn about what is important to you and how you would live from such an exercise? You can skip the year long experiment and do it now in your mind. Put death on your shoulder and walk around with him for a day. Notice what your priorities are. What is most important, most sacred, most cherished? Next, imagine how, when you are aware of your true priorities, you would balance your time?

❈ ❈ ❈ ❈ ❈

Why are we running so fast to feel exhausted, dissatisfied, and empty? Why do we put the means before the ends, the cart before the horse? Why do we lose ourselves in the process of work and labor, and forget the whole?

People who feel they do not have "enough time" are those who experience work as interfering with their personal and family lives. With great respect to the hard workers of the world, this perspective is again a matter of misplaced priorities rather than insufficient time. We all have the same amount of time in a day and we all make choices about how to allocate it. If we choose to spend a disproportionate amount of time at work, that is a choice and we must take responsibility for having given it priority.

Perhaps we prefer work to personal and family time because we are attached to it's rewards, or it is a place where we can avoid the emotional discomfort that arises in our personal life. The world of work, despite its interpersonal difficulties, is less emotionally challenging than the family setting. For many, work is a place to hide from our emotions and the difficult feelings personal and family problems engender.

Workaholism, like alcoholism, is a vehicle for avoiding our feelings. Workaholism, while debilitating and epidemic, is not as well understood as alcoholism and at the same time is socially acceptable, even rewarded, as a positive personal and social characteristic.

Workaholism is the compulsion to continue using work as an escape from the inner life of emotions despite its detrimental effect on our lives. Work, whatever its demands and strains, seldom brings forth the same level of deep seated emotional issues that the family setting generates. The family setting recapitulates the wounds we suffered in our families of origin. And, if we are to be in our current families with joy, we have to feel those uncomfortable feelings and heal from them. Work is a convenient alternative and escape from this painful yet healing process.

Our cultural norms further encourage us not to experience or express our emotions in the work place. Expressing feelings in the work place is seen as unprofessional and inappropriate. We are rewarded for avoiding our emotions and not expressing them. It is a perfect setting to avoid our feelings

If our foremost priority is to experience the joy and harmony that is the birthright of our divinity, then we must live in a way that allows it to emerge. What delivers peace, joy, and balance to all aspects of our lives is attention to and cultivation of the inner experience. When we feel our feelings and remember who we are, then the inner harmony will inevitably result in a balance between work and family life. It is not about moving the furniture but attending to the foundation that allows us to reflect in the world the beauty that lies within.

THE IMPULSE FOR this book came from my work with corporate executives and sales people who had achieved great financial success but were dissatisfied with the lack of balance in their lives. They were an extremely frustrated group. No matter how often or hard they tried, it seemed impossible to catch and hold a proper balance between work and personal life. As we explored the discomfort, it became clear that everyone was focusing at the level of furniture moving.

They tried unsuccessfully to reapportion the time they spent in different segments of their lives, hoping to achieve balance but continually falling short. Though some did make progress, their victories were short lived as their lives soon migrated back to a disproportionate emphasis on work. Even when they succeeded for a time in being more regularly with family, their pleasure was diminished because they were preoccupied with work anyway. They clearly saw the negative impact on themselves and those dearest to them, but like addicts trying to get off their drug, after so many relapses and backsliding, they felt disempowered and hopeless to make a change in their lives.

This reversion to habitual patterns is a law of human nature. It is called "regression to the mean, or "return to homeostasis." When there is only superficial change, behavior will revert to the previously existing habitual patterns which were developed and strengthened over a long period of time. They cut a deep rut into one's psyche and behavior easily falls back into it.

Compulsion and deep-seated habits cannot be overcome with mere resolutions. Fundamental change in the psychological structure that motivates conduct must be addressed for real transformation to occur.

As the group atmosphere among these executive and sales staff progressed, a sense of interpersonal safety evolved and people opened up to share real feelings. In doing so, we arrived at the same conclusion: The reason they could not find a satisfactory balance between family and work was because they were not harmonious within themselves. I did not teach this; I learned it from them.

The source of their dissatisfaction came to be seen not as a problem of juggling work and family but more fundamentally as an imbalance between their inner and outer lives. The outer focus was totally dominant. Their inner focus, aside from worry, was almost absent. They were not nourishing themselves, so they could not nourish their families. It became obvious to us all that the place to start, and the only place that could really make a difference, was at the level of Self. We learned together that the priority must first be coming into inner harmony and then spreading that balance into the rest of our lives.

When we applied Jung's fourfold model of physical, mental, emotional and spiritual components of the self to the discussion, it became clear that they were not nurturing themselves in a complete and integrated way. They were partially taking care of their physical needs, that is the survival needs of housing and food, but few were attending to the temple of their bodies. They did not nurture its needs for movement, exercise, or proper nutrition.

Similarly, they were partially attending to the mental component through the intellectual challenge provided by their work. But they were not feeding other critical aspects of the mind through study and contemplation of the fundamental philosophical questions of life.

Spiritually, some were involved in religious observance, but few had any consistent ongoing spiritual practice. Ritual observance without attending to the more central matter of our direct contact with the divine is not enough to feed the Spirit.

Emotionally they felt at the mercy of their feelings. None were aware of, or understood, the value of honoring feelings as a doorway to insight and liberation.

In our time together, these executives and sales people did some powerful work. The groups became vehicles for profound personal growth. As people who had reached the pinnacle of "success," they knew they were not really successful human beings. Full and complete success was still ahead through the practice of their inner work. This prospect many found exciting and vivifying. It was a very moving experience to be in the presence of this unfolding and it motivated me to write this book.

Beyond the tension between work and personal life, other apparent polarities arise to challenge our sense of balance. There is sometimes a tension between the need for activity and the need for rest. Between action and quiet, or more fundamentally between *doing* and *being*.

With the cultural emphasis so skewed towards doing, there is a great hunger among us for simple being; quiet time to do nothing, be with ourselves and rest in the calm of no-thing. A time without activity, planning, and responsibility. A time to sink into silence, to bathe fully in the peace below the surface. This is fundamental to the process of coming into balance because cultivating the inner life requires islands of quiet within the daily bustle.

The handmaid of silence is solitude. We all need time alone to turn towards the Source. "Free time" cannot all be allotted between work and family because, if it is, the well of balance which allows both to flourish goes dry. In order to nurture the state of being in which the inner life can grow, solitude is a necessary constituent.

THERE IS AN EVEN greater need for alone time among the very active. I am reminded of Winston Churchill, a man who was as active as any in the twentieth century, who knew how important quiet and solitude are in nourishing greatness. Even in the midst of running a nation during a terrible world war, he never missed his quiet and alone time every day so that inside he would be rested and renewed to perform his responsibilities.

Being alone, or in the quiet companionship of another, in nature is perhaps the best antidote to our over dependence on doing. It is as if the creation has provided us the perfect setting to counterbalance the activity of our busy lives. Quiet time in nature, letting the passing dramas and machinations of the mind come to rest, gives us a perspective that aligns the elements of our lives into a healthy orderly whole. We see from the lofty perspective of nature that while some of our life challenges, like ill health and death, are real, most of our problems are self-generated and exacerbated by anxiety and worry. There are few problems in life that cannot be diminished by a long enough walk on the beach.

Creating a proper balance between work and family life, doing and being, solitude and togetherness is not a problem solving or mechanical operation. It is an organic process. We bring the whole into balance so that the parts are in harmony.

one act play

we are all characters in the one act play
"my current confusion."

written, starring and directed
by me.

sometimes we sit together and chat
warm drinks
gracious feelings
living what is
forgetting "what could be"

we leave the drama
live without scripts
abandon set scenes
improvising

soon major themes recur:
work/money
health/security
success/power/fame.

the inner director shouts
"pay attention
believe deeply. . ."
sucked in again by drama

compelled to solve problems
only clarity will do in this one act play

there is not resolution
at the level of illusion

only stepping down
from the stage
  · into the Center

abandon Hollywood!

Once we understand that outer balance flows naturally from inner harmony, our number one priority becomes clear. We adjust and measure the appropriateness of our behavior against whether it serves the development of our higher Self. If we are confused about how we should act or allocate our time, we use this priority as our guide. We ask the question, "Does this further my priority or not?" If it does, we do it; if it doesn't, we let it go. If we are still not clear, we choose either alternative and check in with ourselves later to see if it has served our highest goals and how to handle such situations the next time they arise.

A great help in this process is learning to develop strong personal boundaries around the choices we make based on our priorities. The larger society—represented by friends, work mates, family and cultural models—seldom has a clear sense of what really counts in life. As a result, they try to influence us toward their unexamined priorities, because unconsciously it makes them more comfortable to see us in the same confusion and imbalance as they are. If we do not have strong boundaries protecting our choices, and the ability and willingness to say no to what disturbs our internal harmony, we will slip back into discord and imbalance. We need to learn to resist the pressures of, "do this," "don't do that," "what's the matter with you?" and find the strength to say "no" to people or societal pressures that are pulling us back toward an unprioritized life.

There is a price to pay for saying no. A price to pay for saying no to family and friends, work mates, and bosses when they seek to invade our boundaries. That price, however, is not as costly as a life out of balance.

A harmonious life will sometimes be disappointing to others. By choosing harmony—a life that is joyful and balanced between work and family, doing and being, community and solitude—you will inevitably disappoint some in your circle. But it is a temporary setback, one that is offset by the delight of running free.

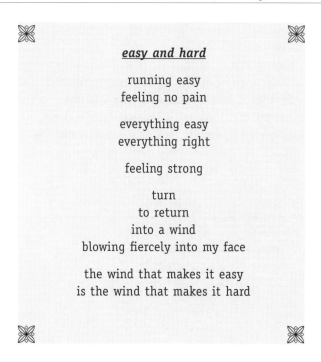

easy and hard

running easy
feeling no pain

everything easy
everything right

feeling strong

turn
to return
into a wind
blowing fiercely into my face

the wind that makes it easy
is the wind that makes it hard

Family, Work, and Money

LIVING SIMPLY IS an invaluable aid in the journey toward wholeness. If we become captured by attachment to material acquisition, if we let it become an end rather than a means to support our inner development, then balance will remain elusive. If we spin our wheels in the process of accumulation, the body of our behavior will not support the head of our true aspirations.

So many people in our society who desire harmony and balance get lost in accumulation. They begin with the intention to create a material context that will serve their goal of personal happiness, but once in the struggle forget the goal. They get side tracked by the game and develop the illusion that the process is the goal.

But in the end it doesn't work. Material comfort and the fulfillment of our physical needs cannot make the inner life more accessible. Obsession with material acquisition makes balance impossible. While we are attending to our material needs we must also attend to that which sustains inner harmony. Attachment to material things obscures our priorities. Accumulation is a diversion from the real work of living.

The accumulation of things does not bring us happiness, but the appreciation of them does. Its not in the owning of things that satisfaction develops, but in the savoring of them. We don't need much to be happy. True joy is in the basics. Awakening and going to sleep. Tastes, touch, smells, sounds, sights, and the experience of love.

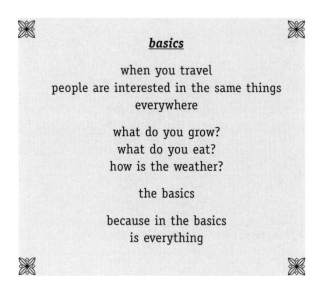

basics

when you travel
people are interested in the same things
everywhere

what do you grow?
what do you eat?
how is the weather?

the basics

because in the basics
is everything

Family life, if we do not complicate it with soap opera drama, is one of these basic earth-real joys. Family life is not about material stuff: plastic toys for the kids, more cars, or a bigger house. It's about heart connections. The love we foster and share with family members it allows us to give and receive more fully.

Family is also about the powerful meaning of lineage and heritage, of being born and fostering children to succeed us. If we remember that our families do not need excesses of material stuff and the superficial fluff of consumer culture but connectedness to truly flourish, then we may be less inclined to get lost in the search for wealth at the expense of our souls.

Spending time outside of our country, we can often see how

many people less well off materially are able to lead richer emotional lives than we Americans.

sunday evening in la pampa

in General Pico
La Pampa
Argentina
i passed a crowded corner

a vacant lot
with a rough fence
and a door
to the carnival inside

families everywhere

white shirts
sparkling
in the moonlight

inside
painted wooden horses
follow and endless path

delighted children scream
grandmothers smile

yellow lights
illuminate faces
of children
staring into the sky
everyone
well combed.

a little girl
reminds me
of my little girl
in a moment of pure knowing
i understand

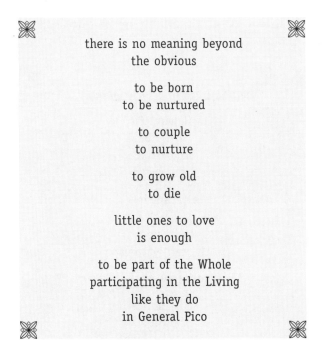

there is no meaning beyond
the obvious

to be born
to be nurtured

to couple
to nurture

to grow old
to die

little ones to love
is enough

to be part of the Whole
participating in the Living
like they do
in General Pico

In *Rekindling the Spirit in Work*, I wrote of the ways in which growing spiritually and emotionally makes our work a richer and happier experience. There I described the ways that consciously experiencing work-related challenges can be a valuable spiritual and emotional practice.

Fundamentally, *Rekindling the Spirit in Work* shows how identifying with our Essence and studying our personal history leads us to discover our special gifts. Over time we can grow our work into an aspect of our lives that satisfies both our material needs and contributes to our overall well being.

Also, when problems arise in work, they can be a catalyst for our personal growth. Insight and freedom emerge when we recognize problems as learning opportunities, and allow ourselves to fully experience the attendant emotional responses. When this approach to "right livelihood" is taken, the world of work becomes a place for our healing.

Work is an integrated part of the larger panorama that is our life. It cannot be separated out and given its own special set of standards. We can't allow our fear about survival, making money, and paying our bills make us adopt standards we would not allow in the rest of our lives. We must have the courage and self-confidence to say no to that which is unacceptable, knowing we will always find a way to take care of ourselves and our family.

The alternative is self-hatred. We may say we put up with boring work or an autocratic boss because "we have to," or because "its work and we need the money." But the fact is we can no more take behavior that is unacceptable from a boss than we can from a friend or a spouse. It is demeaning and we become less. We will lose our self-respect, and that is too precious a price to pay.

We must consider our lives as a whole and apply the same standards throughout the various activities that comprise it.

Work is far more than a job or source of income. What we do influences who and how we are. As with the law of karma, what we do effects who we become.

For most of us, work constitutes a major portion of our day. If we are miserable at work, we are miserable in our lives. Whatever stories we tell ourselves to make it okay, the fact is we can't be happy unless we are happy in our work.

For work to contribute to inner harmony, it needs to flow from who we uniquely are. We need to follow the call of what really turns us on and move in that direction. Our intuition, when it calls us, is the guide in the journey toward satisfying work.

The opportunities for personal growth through work are immense. I recently consulted with a company that was in financial difficulty. To save peoples' jobs, ownership decided to cut everyone's wages, top to bottom including senior management, as a way for everyone to survive and an alternative to layoffs. Most employees supported the strategy aimed at sharing the burden rather making a few carry it all.

Some workers, though, were not able to see beyond the pain and fear this change brought up in them. They attacked the nearest targets: fellow employees, management, and owners. It was clear that beneath the surface of their anger was a conditioned belief that any such strategy must be designed to harm them. Because of their previous work experiences, they were bound to interpret the change as management unfairly benefiting at their expense.

Though the opportunity is seldom taken, the chances to learn about ourselves anew from challenges like these, rather than falling into reflexive reactivity based on fixed concepts, are abundant in the work place. Facing our fear and coming to understand its nature is far more rewarding and ultimately effective than any unexamined knee-jerk reaction.

When situations or people challenge us at work, we cannot just swallow it, rationalize it away, or separate it from of our "real life." If we try, we are kidding ourselves and fostering a malignancy that will grow into the rest of our lives. We must deal with it directly or we will pass the pain on to others close to us without even knowing its source. We need to treat work and the problems it generates as central to our life and respond to work-related probelms as we would any other challenge life presents us: thoughtfully, truthfully, and with integrity.

WORK IS A COMPOUND of two elements: tasks and relationships. My experience has shown time and again that the ability to do the task element of work is seldom the problem. With notable exceptions, most people have the capacity to do the tasks they are responsible for. What becomes problematic are relationships. If we adopt the Healing Relationship model, described in Chapters Nine and Ten, inevitably our relationships at work improve.

The Healing Relationship emphasizes the quality of connectedness between people as the determining factor in whether the relationship will be satisfying and sustain mutual growth. To improve the quality of relationships we need to focus not on changing the other, but on raising the plane of our own attitudes. Whatever the difficulties, our challenge is to maintain an attitude which supports and empowers the other. Whether we like the other person or not, we move as quickly as our level of consciousness allows to the remembrance that they are at center divine beings. Their negative behavior, just like ours, is the result of previous emotional wounding.

The positive regard that is generated by this behavior is immediately felt by the other. It quickly helps them feel safer and loosens their grip on the destructive reactions of attack and defense. Their energy then becomes available for change and cooperation. If we nurture the seven virtues of the healing relationship, we will improve the quality of our relationships at work and elsewhere. Those seven virtues discussed earlier are:

1. Awareness
2. Truth
3. Acceptance
4. Expression
5. Intuition
6 Intention
7. Nonattachment to outcome

Amongst all the complex things it means to us, work is also play for adults. If you have ever participated in a smoothly functioning effective work team, you have had as an adult the same kind of satisfaction children have at play. In fact, children's games are a form of preparation for adult work roles, just as young animal play is practice for the skills they will need to fend for themselves when mature.

Work can be a primary source for sustaining the camaraderie and creativity we had as children. As an adult, work has the added component of allowing us to feel even deeper satisfaction in supporting others, providing for ourselves and families, and a higher sense of accomplishment. Work can be a place where we bask in the joy of challenge and learning as we did when we were children, only we have the added benefit of what every child wants, being a "grown up."

Work is a central source of meaning in most peoples lives. Seeing the fruits of our efforts is a joy and a counter weight to the tendency of mind to dwell in worry. As the great South African writer Laurens van der Post said, "Meaning transfigures all, and once what you are living and what you are doing has for you meaning, it is irrelevant whether you are happy or unhappy. You are content. You're not alone in your Spirit. You belong."

All work, even the most apparently mundane, can be meaningful if we bring to it a spirit of mindfulness. Each job we do or have builds upon the previous one in teaching us more than any formal education ever will.

There is a beautiful scene in the movie "The English Patient," set during war time, where an army nurse stays behind in dangerous territory when the rest of the troops are withdrawing. She stays to continue caring for her patient, a burn victim. Someone asks why, when she could easily retreat to safety, she would stay? She replies simply, "Because I am a nurse." The power and clarity that comes with following one's calling gives such profound meaning to our lives that the normal confusions of most people, even when multiplied by the existence of danger, comes to nothing in the face of meaningful work.

Too often the lust for power and fame interferes with integrating our life and work. The search for power and public recognition, though they are strong motivators in many of us, usually arises from an inner sense of deficiency. Somehow, due to our life history, our more than sufficient innate authority and love does not consciously shine through to satisfy our need for power and recognition.

When we know ourselves as Essence, we know that we are fully empowered, loved, and recognized just as we are. We feel no need to seek it from the outside. When we know that we are the source of our own love, we do not care about, or need, recognition, fame, or any external proof of love.

Those who succeed in gaining power or fame are seldom satisfied by it. What they have gained does not actually satisfy the deeper longing which has been driving them. The real underlying quest is to know that we are already fully empowered and loved without the necessity to demonstrate domination or superiority. We can save ourselves a lot of drama by focusing our energy on waking up rather than wrestling with trying to achieve what we already have.

<u>after visiting the museum of mankind</u>

i'm humbled
by the work of millions

generations of artists
craftsmen
since the beginning
beauty through the hands

ancient cultures
working in wood
and stone
playing with line
and time
and circles

adorning the routine
with the wonderful

spontaneous and controlled
in fun and earnest
man's storehouse of beauty

some ancient work
still remains
to remind us
there is nothing new

marks are made by chance
what is important
what endures
is the Work

May the expansion of your internal harmony symbolized by the planet Jupiter, support the growth of balance in your life, so magnificently embodied in the beauty of her rings.

About

WHITE CLOUD PRESS

White Cloud Press publishes books on religion and myth,
focusing on the great faith traditions and mystical works.
The press serves as an interfaith resource center for people
looking for spiritual food for thought.
Our books feature some of the best and most inspiring works on
religion available from contemporary writers,
translations of scripture, and classic spiritual texts.

The image of the White Cloud was adopted for the press
because it is a universal image that appears
with different meanings in all cultures and religions.

We invite you to explore worlds of faith through the books of
White Cloud Press.

For more information on all full line of titles,
please visit our web site at
www.whitecloudpress.com

Books to Expand Your Spiritual Horizons

Approaching the Qur'án: The Early Revelations
Translated with an Introduction by Michael Sells
(Quality Paperback with Audio CD / $21.95)

A timely publication that introduces the sacred book of Islam. Hailed by scholars as the best English translation of the Qur'an available today. Includes a 70-minute audio CD of Qur'an reciters.

"Michael Sells has performed an invaluable service in making the beauty, spiritual energy, and compelling power of the Qur'an accessible to a Western audience for the first time." ~ **Karen Armstrong, author of *A History of God***

....

Ways in Mystery: Explorations in MysticalAwareness & Life
Luther Askeland (Quality Paperback / $17)

Ways in Mystery brings together six remarkable essays on the mystical life by Luther Askeland.

"Luther Askeland has brought forth a truly remarkable book, unlike anything this reader has ever encountered. . . . He speaks out of experience that renders a realm, not universally accessible, beautifully transparent."
~ **Joan Stambaugh, author of *The Finitude of Being***

". . . full of grace, profound insight and wisdom." ~ **Publishers Weekly**

"In clear direct language, Askeland explores the most profound questions of the mystical life." ~ **Booklist**

White Cloud books are available from most bookstores or by can be ordered by phone (800-380-8286) or from our web site

White Cloud Press • PO Box 3400 • Ashland, OR 97520
www. whitecloudpress.com

Wisdom Literature

Bridging the I System: Unifying Spirituality and Behavior
Stanley Block, MD, with Carolyn Bryant Block
(Quality Paperback: $15.95)

"In this remarkable work, **Stanley Block** moves toward the outer frontier of present-day wisdom, philosophy, and ontology by pointing out how we mortals severely handicap ourselves by our unwitting submission to the unconscious dictates of the "I-System. *Bridging the I-System* is a dramatic and vital work. I recommend it for . . .. all who seek to unify spirituality and behavior." **~ James G. Grotstein, M.D. is author of "*Who Is the Dreamer Who Dreams the Dream?*" He is Professor of Psychiatry, UCLA School of Medicine and a Training and Supervising analyst both at the Los Angeles Psychoanalytic Institute and at The Psychoanalytic Center of California.**

....

Yin Yoga: Outline of a Quiet Practice
Paul Grilley (Quality Paperback: $15.95)

Yoga as practiced in the US is almost exclusively Yang or muscular in nature. The Yin aspect of Yoga (using postures that stretch connective tissue) is virtually unknown but vital for a balanced approach to physical and mental health. Paul Grilley's *YIN YOGA* outlines how to practice postures in a Yin way.

....

Welcome to the Family! Opening Doors to the Jewish Experience
Lois Shenker (Quality Paperback: $14.95)

"Shenker, an interfaith educator and lifelong Jew, was moved to write this book when three of her children married non-Jews. To make her new family members—and others—feel comfortable understanding Judaism and attending services, this book provides basic information about Jewish beliefs, history, practices, holidays and life-cycle rituals. . . . [T]he book is presented with such kindness and warmth that readers will feel that they, too, have been welcomed into the family." **~Publishers Weekly**

"Welcome to the Family! fills a gap that much needs filling. Ms. Shenker provides all who wish to be included with a truly user-friendly guide to the Jewish heritage." **~ Egon Mayer, Ph.D., Director of Research, Jewish Outreach Institute, Director of Jewish Studies, CUNY**

Books to Expand Your Spiritual Horizons

Everything Starts from Prayer: Mother Teresa's Meditations on Spiritual Life for People of All Faiths

Mother Teresa, With a Foreword by Larry Dossey, M.D.
(Quality Paperback: $12.95 / Cloth: $17.95)

Everything Starts from Prayer is the first book of its kind, simultneously offering Mother Teresa's spiritual guidance and providing a step-by-step introduction to prayer.

"Mother Teresa was one of the great spiritual servants of our era, whose simple wisdom expressed untold depths of devotion. In this treasury of her thoughts on prayer, she offers the world another blessing." ~ **President Jimmy Carter**

....

The Green Sea of Heaven: Fifty ghazals from the Díwán of Háfiz

Shams al-Dín Muhammad Háfiz-i Shirází
Translated by Elizabeth T. Gray, Jr. (Quality Paperback / $15.95)

"This is a groundbreaking work, one that places the ghazal of Háfiz into a contemporary English poetic idiom. Ms. Gray captures the rhythms, the paradoxes, the ironies, the sudden changes in tone and voice, the ambiguities, the spark and the bite of the original. After too long a wait, we encounter Háfiz, come alive in an English style that is at once natural and intricate. This is a remarkable achievement."
~ **Michael Sells, author of *Mystical Languages of Unsaying***

....

SAGA: Best New Writings on Mythology, vol. 2

Edited by Jonathan Young (Quality Paperback / $15.95)

Jonathan Young follows up his highly acclaimed first volume of *SAGA* with a remarkable collection of essays on mythology and ritual. Contributors include **Jean Houston** on "*Mythic Possiblities*," **Angeles Arrien** on "*The Way of the Tribe*," **Robert Sardello** on "*The Love of Soul and the Healing of the World*," **Carol P. Christ** on "*The Serprentine Path*," **Jacob Needleman** on "*Why We Argue*," and **Michael Ventura** on "*Rats from a Sinking Ship*."